Classification of the Animal Kingdom

Classification
of the Animal Kingdom

An Introduction to Evolution

Kenneth Jon Rose

David McKay Company, Inc.
New York

Library of Congress Cataloging in Publication Data

Rose. Kenneth Jon.
  Classification of the animal kingdom.

  Includes index.
  SUMMARY: This introduction to evolution discusses the classification system used to arrange members of the animal kingdom.
  1. Zoology—Classification—Juvenile literature. 2. Evolution—Juvenile literature. [1. Zoology—Classification. 2. Evolution] I. Title.
QL351.R67   591'.012   79-3465
ISBN 0-679-20508-X

  3 4 5 6 7 8 9 10

Manufactured in the United States of America

To Ben
. . . thanks.

CONTENTS

Classification of the Animal Kingdom

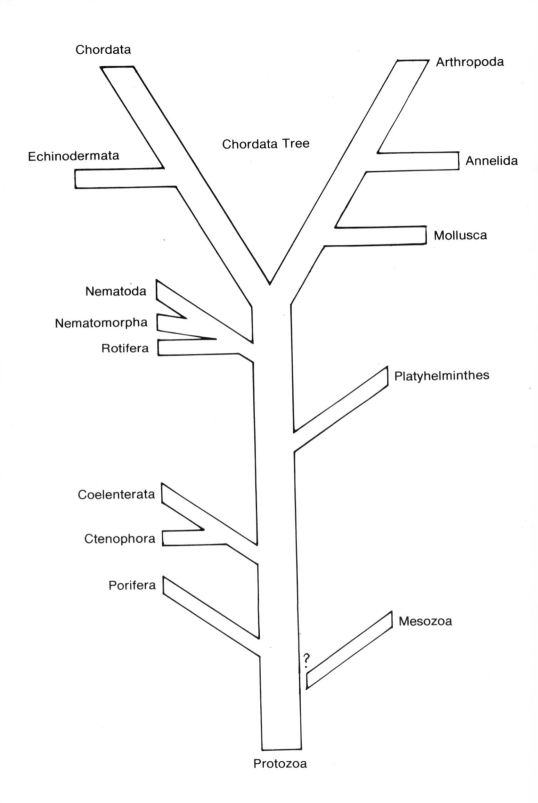

The First Step

We are swimming in an unusual ocean. It may not *look* very unusual, but the fact is, the sea is some three billion years old. And there is a unique event occurring here.

The first animals ever to appear on this earth are in the water with us. But we can't see them, at least not with the naked eye. They are too small—smaller, in fact, than the period at the end of this sentence.

If we had brought along a microscope, we would have seen that they are quite different from their one-celled neighbors, the plants. Unlike the casually drifting plants, the single-celled animals lack the green pigment, called chlorophyll ('klor-uh-fil), involved in making food from sunlight. Because of this disadvantage, they have to actively seek out their food—the plants and the other animals around them. Otherwise, they would die.

Compared to us, they are not very complex creatures. Many of them look like tiny glass footballs, filled with cloudy gelatin. Attached to their bodies are thin, whiplike tails—the flagella (flah-'jel-uh)—that push or pull the animals around the warm waves. Other one-celled creatures look like they are covered with short hairs, or *cilia*. These propel the creatures through the water.

Who would think that these tiny, one-celled animals evolved into the millions of different varieties of animals we see today and the untold millions of those that died off without a trace?

Yet, for all their variety, they are not so different from one another. The earliest people knew this when they found that, for their own survival, they could place the animals around them into groups. There were wormlike beings, bugs, and animals with hair on their bodies. Even more important, people discovered that there were some animals they could eat—and some that could eat them!

But people are not the only ones who group animals. All animals put other organisms into groups. For a fish, there are the two important groups: food and nonfood. For a fly, there can be competitors and potential mates. For a lizard, there are enemies and prey.

This grouping—placing animals into groups on the basis of their relationships—is called *classification.*

How It Began

During his life, Aristotle, the great Greek philosopher and biologist (384–322 B.C.), studied many animals, including those in and around the sea. From his observations, he learned that the animals he saw could be grouped, or classified, by what they had in common. "Animals," he wrote, "may be characterized according to their way of living, their actions, their habits, and their bodily parts."

It was this kind of thinking that brought Aristotle to form several major groupings of animals, many that are still used today: birds, fishes, whales, and insects. But he also saw that even these groups could be broken down into smaller ones. Aristotle found animals to be two-footed or four-footed, hairy or feathered, with or without shells, and even blooded or bloodless. Needless to say, he was very perceptive for his time.

Unfortunately, Aristotle did not always place animals into the correct groups. Sometimes he placed an animal that looked very similar to another into the same group. Ordinarily, such a mistake would have been corrected by another biologist later in history. But Aristotle's influence was so great that no one dared question his work. It was never questioned until 2000 years after his death!

It might have dawned on him, when he was sitting on the shore of the Aegean Sea, that there was a pattern to the kinds of animals he had grouped. Many of them, he thought, were less perfect than others. Why not categorize them that way?

Aristotle also believed that, because plants had no soul and no motivation to do anything (they never moved), they were the lowest of living things and, therefore, the least perfect forms (besides the soil and rocks) in the world. Animals, he believed, were more perfect than plants simply because they reacted to life. And, within the animal kingdom itself, there were some creatures that were more perfect than others.

From this theory, he began to envision a scale, and he started to arrange animals into a *scala naturae*, or natural scale, according to their degree of perfection. It was this scale that led to the more developed science of *taxonomy*.

Taxonomy is a combination of two Greek words: *taxis*, meaning arrangement, and *nomos*, meaning law. Simply put, taxonomy is the science of classifying organisms.

The Swedish naturalist, Carolus Linnaeus, born in 1707, was the first to put taxonomy into widespread use in biology. Different types of classification systems were cropping up all over the world, making it very difficult for anyone to see what any one system had in common with another.

Linnaeus' interest in classification began when he was only eight years old. His family even dubbed him "the little botanist." For hours on end, he studied the flowers around his home and observed what made one flower different from another.

In Linnaeus' lifetime, a great many animals and plants were discovered during trips made by European explorers. A system was needed to make it easier for biologists to keep track of what the explorers had found. Linnaeus set out to make such a system.

How, he thought, can I group the animals in the best way? He solved the problem, and his solutions appeared in the first edition of his book, *Systema Naturae* (Natural System).

In this book, Linnaeus divided the animal kingdom into six large groups: quadrupeds *(quadri,* four; *ped,* foot; or animals with four feet), with hairy bodies, that can produce milk; birds; amphibia (am-'fib-ee-uh), animals that spend part of their lives in water, such as the frogs; fishes; insects; and worms.

Like Aristotle, Linnaeus grouped together only animals that he believed were related. And, according to the Swedish taxonomist, snails and a great many shellfish, as well as hundreds of microorganisms, were put into the worm group. It was not until years after his death that these creatures were put into the correct categories.

Even though the "Father of Taxonomy" was incorrect about some of his groups, he was way ahead of his time when he suggested that man and ape should be in the same category. He saw that they had numerous traits in common. But many times his desk was filled with angry letters from people who believed that Man should not be included with the rest of the animals.

Linnaeus, however, was a religious man. He firmly believed that the world was the work of God, and his religious beliefs came through in his work. The naturalist felt that the way animals were arranged—from the most primitive creatures to the highest, ourselves—was the plan of creation. To Linnaeus, the animals he saw on farms and in the ocean were the same as they were when God put them on Earth. Each animal was like a separate unit that never changed. Linnaeus' views were typical of the times and accepted by most other scientists as facts. It was not until 100 years later that this view was discarded.

In 1859, another naturalist, Charles Darwin, wrote a famous book, *The Origin of Species,* which changed people's
ways of thinking about themselves and about the world
around them. Darwin wrote that animals *evolved* from other
animals through *evolution.* Animals, he observed, were not
units that were separate from one another, but were constantly changing into other forms. Animals were similar not
because they had some traits in common but because they
had evolved from the same ancestor.

This view understandably created a big stir at the time
because it challenged the religious thinking of the day.
Nevertheless, after many bitter battles, evolution became a
widely accepted theory.

Interestingly, Darwin's book did little to alter the structure of the classification system. It did, however, change its
meaning. Taxonomy was no longer just a way of organizing
animals into groups because of their looks. Now the animals
were arranged according to their background—that is, what
animals they had evolved from. This method of dealing with
taxonomy is still used today.

The Needed Parts

Before a classification system could really be used, the
animals involved had to be given names. Now this may
sound ridiculous because all of the animals already had
names. But what was really needed were names that would
be universally used and understood.

Linnaeus thought about this problem when he was
working on his classification system, and he came up with the
perfect answer: Latin names. During his day, the letters of all
men of learning were written in Latin. Because it was a
"dead" language—one that was not then actively used by any
civilization (the Ancient Romans who had used it many cen-
turies ago were all gone)—it would never change. Linnaeus
knew that such a language was also very important because

it would be accepted throughout the world by everyone who worked in scientific fields.

But something else would be needed. Years before Linnaeus' time, taxonomists used long descriptions to identify the animals. A taxonomist might have described the red-faced warbler as "a bird that is gray above, white below, with bright-red forehead, throat, and breast, and with white rump." Linnaeus decided that only two words were really needed to identify an animal (or a plant), and he used what is now called the *binomial* system of *nomenclature*.

What that garble of letters means is simply this: nomenclature ('nō-'muhn-klā-chuhr) is the act of naming; binomial *(bi,* two; *nomin,* name) represents two names. In other words, Linnaeus gave each type of animal a name in two parts. For instance, modern man, in Linnaeus' system, is *Homo sapiens,* meaning literally "man wise."

This binomial name is also the *scientific name* for an animal. Each part of the name is important for identification; both parts are governed by a strict set of rules on how they will be used.

The first part, or *generic* name, always has its first letter capitalized. The second part, or *specific* name, does not. Both are underlined (italicized) because they are foreign words.

Sometimes two different scientific names for the same animal are found because two or more people, each from a different country, didn't get together in their work. In these cases, the earliest name is used.

The rules say that if the name is in Latin it can be used in the system. Therefore, many names are taken from the scientist's native language and Latinized. This means that a Latin ending is added to the word.

How Taxonomy Works

The taxonomic system is a graded, or ranked, series,

known as a *hierarchy*. What is meant by a hierarchy? Let's use a very familiar example to illustrate this: Suppose we walk into a supermarket. What is the first choice of items we make? Do we want food or nonfood? We almost always make this choice without having to think about it. Thus we have formed the two largest categories: food and nonfood.

Right away, we can make another choice: Do we want a meat or a vegetable? These two lesser categories can fit into the category of food.

But now we're a little more choosy. In the meat department, there's a wide selection to pick from: lamb, pork, veal, beef, and chicken. All of them fit nicely into the larger category of meats.

We pick beef. But there's another choice to make. Within the beef section, there are prime ribs, sirloin, London broil, and hamburger. We choose hamburger.

Finally, we have to make still another choice—whether we want chopped sirloin, or ground round.

So we see that we can represent our choices in a ranked series that becomes more and more specific:

food
meat
beef
hamburger
ground round

We can do the same sort of thing with the animal kingdom.

Linnaeus was the first taxonomist to put the kingdom into a clear hierarchy of categories. Later, others refined his system. Today, animals are arranged into seven well-known categories, in which *phylum* ('fī-luhm) is the highest and *species* the lowest.

The basic taxonomic hierarchy looks like this:

Kingdom
Phylum
Class
Order
Family
Genus
Species

The entire animal kingdom is first divided into large categories called *phyla* (the plural of phylum). The animals that make up a phylum live in every part of the environment and differ in size and behavior. Yet the one thing that they have in common is their basic structure.

Take, for instance, the phylum *Arthropoda*. This group includes lobsters, all insects, spiders, and millipeds. Their one common structure is that their bodies are divided into segments, and their legs are jointed. No other phylum has this body structure.

The individual phyla are then divided into numerous *classes*. Each class is usually separated from the others by its particular way of life. In other words, the Class Amphibia is different from the Class Aves (birds) in that Amphibia (even though they both belong to the phylum Chordata) spend much of their lives in the water. The Class Aves does not.

Classes are further divided into *orders*. One order is still different enough to be seen as separate from another order. The Order Insectivora (insect eaters)—the shrews and the moles—differ from the Order Chiroptera (finger wings, or bats)—even though both belong to the class Mammalia (a group that has hair and nurses its young with milk). The bat is a *flying* mammal.

Members of one *family* can be separated from another by their particular niche, or individual place in the world. For instance, a worm-eating bird with a long, slender bill, would find it very difficult to take the place of a bird that eats only hard-shelled nuts. The worm-eater's beak would not be powerful enough to crack nutshells; it would need a short, thick bill to do the job. But both kinds of birds might be in the same order.

Families are further divided into *genera* (the singular is genus). You will notice that the genus is also the first part of the scientific name given to an animal. Even if there is a "gap" between one genus and another, the gap is often so small that it is almost unnoticeable to the untrained eye. The crayfish of the genus *Cambarus* has seventeen pairs of gills; the genus *Astacus* has eighteen. If they were to suddenly trade places with each other, they would probably survive just as well.

Finally, we come to the last category in the taxonomic hierachy: the species. *Species* are not individual animals, but *populations* of animals. When we speak of species, we speak of the species of Canadian Goose, *Branta canadensis*, or the species of modern man, *Homo sapiens*. In other words, when we mention a species, we are including *all* of the individuals in that species.

A species is one that can only breed successfully within its own population. Many times, two species in the same genus may look almost identical and may have the exact same structure, but they will not be able to mate successfully with each other because of some very minor, but *very important*, differences. For example, two species of crickets may look exactly the same, yet their chirps may be completely different. Because the females of one species do not respond to the call of another, the two species never mate, even if they are standing next to each other. This makes them a separate species.

Sometimes you will see a scientific name with three Latin words, such as *Rattus rattus rattus*, the common rat. The third word simply means that it is a variety, or race, in the species. Dogs are a good example of this. There are Irish setters, German shepherds, Boston terriers, Basset hounds, and many other breeds, but they all belong to the same species, *Canis familiaris.* The only ways in which they really differ from one another is in their outward appearances.

The Next Step

In the beginning of this book, you probably noticed the tree diagram, with the names of different phyla on the branches. Although this was meant to be of some help in keeping the animal kingdom straight in your mind, the diagram was also included to indicate the ancestry of the animal groups. Those toward the trunk are the most primitive animals—not because they are simple in their shapes or uncomplicated in their way of life. They represent a time in history, when they lived and survived to evolve into other, more successful forms, like ourselves.

Beyond the First Animal

2

PHYLUM

PROTOZOA (prod-uh-'zo-uh)

(first animals)

Protozoa are everywhere—in lakes, streams, and oceans; on trees and in the soil; inside snails and worms; and even inside you.

To taxonomists, Protozoa are the link to the past billions of years ago when animals first evolved from the most primitive plants. Yet, for all their importance, no one knows quite how to categorize them.

To be a member of the phylum Protozoa, an animal must be self-sufficient and single-celled. But not all of the Protozoa are alike. There are some that are large enough to be seen with the unaided eye and others that are so small they can only be studied under a powerful microscope. Some get their food from the sun and some, the parasites, feed on other animals. There are those that move by their flagella and those that move by extending part of their body like false feet (pseudopodia). And there are still others that don't move at all from the stone they're attached to.

Needless to say, all of these variations make it very difficult for taxonomists to categorize them. Some biologists have even put the phylum Protozoa in their own separate kingdom. But Protozoa has been included in this book with the rest of the animals so that you will be able to see the transition from these single-celled forms to the many-celled animals that evolved after them.

There are four classes included in this phylum: Flagellata (creatures that use long, whiplike organs for movement), Rhizopodia (animals that move by extending their bodies), Sporozoa (animals that live in another animal and reproduce by spores), and Ciliata (animals that move by their cilia).

Class FLAGELLATA (flajuh-'lahd-uh)

These animals are the most primitive of the four classes because they are probably the ancestors of animals that evolved from the plants. Some even contain the green pigment necessary to get food from sunlight. They could be called plants, and some botanists put many of them into the plant kingdom. The members of this class may contain one or more flagella and are usually free-living, although many are parasitic. Most are shaped like the shells of chicken eggs.

Order EUGLENIDA (yoo-'gleen-uhduh)

These animals are shaped like partially deflated footballs. Their bodies are not rigid, but change slightly, like balloons filled with water. Depending on the species, these freshwater creatures have one or two flagella that emerge from a pit in their body. Many make their own food from the sun, which is why some biologists claim that these animals should be in the plant kingdom. But there are also those that eat other animals for nourishment.

FAMILY EUGLENIDAE (yoo-'gleen-uh-dee)

This family contains all of the euglenids that make their food from sunlight.

Genus *Euglena* (yoo-'gleen-uh)

All *Euglena* live in fresh water and get their food from

the sun, which is why they are green. From a long gullet, gouged along the body, is a long flagellum that whips about in the water, pulling the animal forward while it spins around like a fish lure. Also within the body is a tiny bit of material that is very sensitive to light. Called an eyespot, it directs the animal to light, where it is then able to feed.

Species *E. gracilis*

These animals are shaped like a cylinder.

Species *E. spirogyra*

These creatures have a large, flattened body.

Order KINETOPLASTIDA (keh-'nee-duh-plastuh-duh)

The strange name given to this order simply means that the animal contains a kinoplast—a specialized part of the cell that has material that influences the movement of the body. The animals included in this order may have anywhere from one to four flagella. Most of them are parasitic, inhabiting the blood or the intestines of other animals.

FAMILY TRYPANOSOMATIDAE (treh-panuh-so-'mad-uh-dee)

All of these animals have a long, slender flagellum and are parasitic. Many of them may change their forms during their life cycles.

Genus *Trypanosoma* (treh-panuh-'somuh) (borer)

Trypanosoma, parasites of the blood, live part of their lives within many vertebrates, such as birds, reptiles, amphibians, fish, and mammals (including people). The other part of their lives are spent within the stomachs of blood-sucking animals like the flea and the tsetse fly.

Species *T. gambiense*

This species is the cause of a great deal of pain and

suffering for people in southern Africa because it is the cause of a form of sleeping sickness. *T. gambiense* is transmitted by the tsetse fly (genus *Glossina*). Almost all of the wild game in Africa carry these tiny flagellates in their blood. When a tsetse fly sucks the blood of an infected animal, the small creatures are drawn into the stomach of the fly. There they change into another form and multiply. When one of the infected flies bites a person, the one-celled animals are injected into the blood and again multiply. Because they give off waste products as they multiply, the build-up of the material can cause fever; and when they move up around the spine of a person, it can cause death. Great efforts have been made to get rid of the flies so that the flagellates can't complete their life cycles, but so far, scientists have not been very successful.

Order   DINOFLAGELLIDA (dino-fluh-'jeluh-duh)

The name comes from the Greek, *dinos,* meaning whirling and terrible. The dinoflagellates have the characteristics of both plants and animals. Some get their nourishment from the sun, others by eating animals. Still others are parasites, feeding on their host for food. Most of the species live in the sea, but there are some that live in lakes and ponds. The majority of the flagellates have rigid armor, or "tests," around their bodies; many look like dented boxes, with the edges and corners crushed in. Around the middle of the animal is a groove, where a long, thin flagellum lies like a belt. Another flagellum trails behind the animal.

Dinoflagellates are responsible for much of the tiny lights in the seawater at night. If you ever row a boat in the sea on a summer night, you may see small, quick flashes of light, like dancing fireflies, around the hull. These may be from the animals in this order. Most are colored. In fact, the Red Sea got its name from the red-colored dinoflagellates.

FAMILY   NOCTILUCIDAE (nahktuh-'lookuh-dee)

Genus *Noctiluca* (nahk-tuh-'lookuh) (lantern)

These animals, only as thick as a penny, are phosphorescent. They sometimes appear in great numbers, called "blooms," where they make the ocean glow at night and give the water a red tint by day. *Noctiluca* feed on other animals.

Species *N. scintillans*

This is one of the largest of the *Noctiluca* and the most common offshore. They get their name from the fact that after one of them flashes, the water suddenly sparkles with millions of individual lights, then becomes dark again.

FAMILY GONIAULIDAE (gōnee-'ah-laduh-ee)

Genus *Gonyaulax* (gonee-'aw-laks)

One of the more interesting of the dinoflagellates is the genus *Gonyaulax*. When many of them get together in one place, the ocean can be a rotten spot to spend the summer. The animals are shaped very much like *Noctiluca*. They have tight-fitting armor around their bodies and two flagella—one lying in a groove encircling the animal, the other trailing downward. When they multiply in great numbers (one quart of water can contain some 5 million of them), what is known as a "red tide" develops. They compete for the oxygen in the water, while at the same time releasing poisonous material from their bodies that kills thousands of fish.

Species *G. catanella*

The waste products of these animals are extremely powerful and highly poisonous. Just one gram of the poison (no more than a couple of drops) can kill 5 million mice in 15 minutes. Some animals, especially the marine mussels, can concentrate a lot of the toxin within their bodies without any bad effects. But many people who eat them, when *Gonyaulax* is in the water, die. The toxin is currently being studied by the Chemical Warfare Division of the U.S. Army.

Class   RHIZOPODEA (rizuh-'podee-uh) (root foot)

Think of a glob of warm jelly sitting on the kitchen counter and you probably have a good idea of what many in the class Rhizopodia look like. Most of these animals move around by extending their bodies, technically called the pseudopodia (false feet), flowing forward to meet them, and then extending more pseudopodia. Some have shells and extend very thin "false feet," like antennae, around their bodies to catch even smaller animals. Others build "tests" around themselves and hide in them whenever they are preyed upon.

Some Rhizopods live in fresh or salt water and in damp soil. Others are parasitic and live in the bodies of larger animals. Many biologists think that Rhizopods may be closely related to the flagellates because, in some of the animals, flagella are present during their early life stages.

Order   AMOEBIDA (uh-'mee-bi-duh) (the changers)

There is no description of these animals that could do justice to their form. They are formless, which makes it very difficult for the taxonomist to place them in the right category. All are without shells and "tests." Most are common to lakes and ponds, but there are some that live in the ocean, and others that are parasitic. Some are very small, and some are rather large—about the diameter of the thickness of three pennies. However, most biologists can distinguish the different species by the shape of their pseudopodia—whether their "false feet" are just for movement or for feeding—and by what is present inside their bodies.

Genus   *Amoeba* (uh-'meebuh)

Perhaps the most famous of the Rhyzopodea, the *Amoeba*, is studied in nearly every science class. These animals are constantly changing shape, extending their rounded, blunt-ended pseudopodea both for movement and for feeding. When a small, one-celled plant (protozoan) or even a very small multicellular organism swims nearby, the amoeba tries to surround the prey with its body. If it succeeds, the food actually becomes trapped within a bubble, or vacuole, made by the closing of the cell membrane around the prey. It is later digested by the amoeba's chemicals.

FAMILY ENDAMOEBIDAE ('ehnt-uh-meebuh-dee)

Genus *Entamoeba* ('ent-uh-meebuh)

These are small amoebas that live inside our bodies. They inhabit the intestine, or the gums around the teeth. Some are harmful, some are helpful.

Species *E. histolytica*

This species, called "dysentery amoeba," is very harmful to us. It occurs in approximately 5 to 10 percent of the developed countries, and in 60 percent of the underdeveloped countries, such as some nations in South America and Africa. Raw sewage and *E. histolytica* almost go together. When the animal gets into your food or drinking water, it goes right to your large intestine, where it begins feeding on the cells that make up the intestine wall. If there are enough of the animals, they can rupture the lining and cause it to bleed. Once that happens, the organisms can get into your system, feed on the red blood cells, and make you very ill. The way to avoid this is to clean anything that comes into contact with your food.

Order FORAMINIFERIDA (fuh-ramuh-'nif-uh-ruh-duh) (hole-bearers)

You wouldn't think that the foraminiferida were related to the amoebas if you saw one, but they are. When they are young, they look like their bloblike relatives, but they immediately begin secreting a shell around themselves. As they grow, their bodies ooze out of the shell opening and spread over the top of it. Once again, they secrete another shell of chalk over their exposed bodies, making a second chamber. And, as it continues growing, the animal repeats the process until there may be as many as 100 open chambers around the animal. It eventually looks like a snail shell, with long, thin spines jutting out of it like a tiny pincushion. The spines are, in fact, pseudopods that have come out of the pores (remember what Foraminiferida means) ·of the shell. In many of the species, their movements help to capture food.

When they die, only their shells are left, and they fall to the ocean floor. Today, the bottom of the ocean is littered with billions of empty shells, which are very important con-tributors to the sediment of the sea. They are also important to scientists, who can date them for finding oil deposits.

When much of England was under water millions of years ago, empty Foraminiferida shells were deposited in the area of the White Cliffs of Dover. The cliffs are white be-cause of the chalk shells.

FAMILY GLOBIGERINIDAE (glō-bijuh-'rinuh-dee)

Genus *Globigerina* (glow-'bijuh-rin-uh)

Most of the shells now falling to the bottom of the ocean are of this genus. Thirty percent of the ocean floor is covered with them. When they are alive, they float below the waves.

Species *G. bulloides*

This species looks like three or four pincushions glued together.

Class SPOROZOA (spoh-ruh-'zō-uh) (spore-animals)

Each member of this class is a parasite of some other animal. Through millions of years of evolution, they have lost their food entrances and their means of actively swim-ming around. They have developed instead a very complex way of surviving. Many of them get their nutrition by ab-

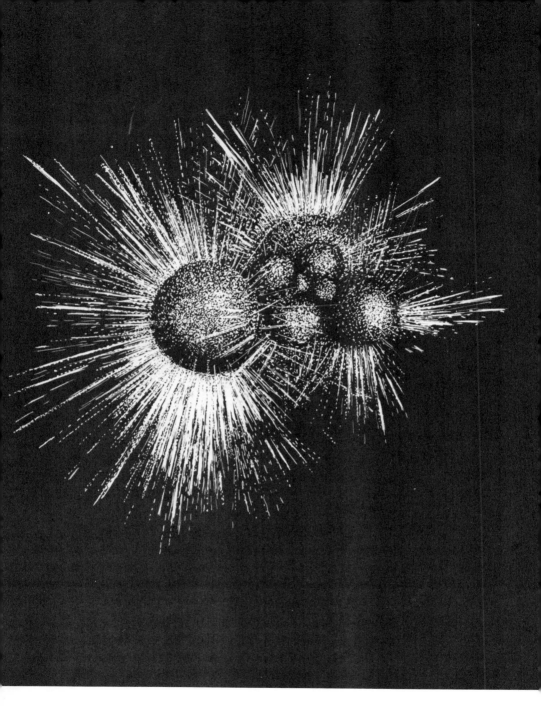

Globigerina, single-celled animals related to the amoeba. They float in the ocean, capturing food in their thin pseudopods. (DRAWING BY LAUREL STERN)

sorbing it through their "skin," or cell membrane. All of them move from one place to another by letting their hosts take them inside their bodies and passing them through to another host.

Sporozoans get their names because of their unique lifestyle. When one of the cells is ready to divide, the nucleus (the part of the cell that controls the cell's functions) divides many times until many nuclei are made. Then the inner fluid of the cell surrounds each nucleus and breaks apart from the others until each is a separate offspring. This process happens inside the host.

While some sporozoa have a resistant covering around them, much like a seed, others do not.

Order   HAEMOSPORIDIA (heemō-spuh-'ridee-uh)

A male and a female mate within the stomach of a blood-sucking insect. When they are injected into a mammal, they break up into spores within their red blood cells by the process described above. They have no resistant covering.

FAMILY   PLASMODIIDAE (plaz-muh-'dīuh-dee)

These animals go through the blood system of mammals and the digestive systems of mosquitoes.

Genus   *Plasmodium* (plaz-'mōdee-uhm)

When soldiers came back from Vietnam, many of them experienced chills and fever that came in waves every two or three days. What they probably were experiencing was malaria, caused by *Plasmodium.*

When the female *Anopheles* (uh-'nahfuh-leez) mosquito bites an infected person (one who has malaria), *Plasmodium* goes right to the stomach of the insect and reproduces many more *Plasmodium.* Then this tiny animal swims to the saliva gland in the mosquito's mouth. When the insect bites a non-infected person, the one-celled animals enter the bloodstream and attack the blood cells. As they reproduce even more, they contaminate the blood with their wastes. This causes the chills and fever.

Plasmodium multiplies every 48 or 72 hours, depending on the species.

Species *P. vivax*

Multiplies every 48 hours.

Class CILIATA (silee-'at-uh) (having an eyelash)

Those tiny animals you see darting around in a drop of water on a slide are probably members of this class. The cilia around their bodies give them speed. In most of the animals, the cilia are so well coordinated with each other that, under a microscope, they seem to beat in waves. One paddles right after the other, like a row of dominoes falling and getting back up again.

Most of these creatures are free-living. But there are a few that attach themselves to nonmoving objects, using their cilia to bring in food. Others are parasitic.

Order HYMENOSTOMATIDA (himuh-no-'stahm-uhd-iduh)

These animals have cilia spaced evenly all around their body. They also have grooves or depressions along their bodies that are surrounded by cilia leading to the mouth.

Genus *Paramecium* (paruh-'meesh-ee-uhm)

Paramecium live in fresh water, especially in quiet pools. These slipper-shaped animals are covered with short, fine hairlike cilia that beat in waves to move the animal backward or forward. Food is swept into a groove along the body. Different species vary in size.

Order PERITRICHIDA (peruh-'tri-kuhduh)

Most of these animals are attached to nonmoving objects by a stalk secreted by the cell. They feed by waving their cilia to bring food to their mouths.

FAMILY   VORTICELLIDAE (vawrd-uh-'seluh-dee)

Genus   *Vorticella* (vawrd-uh-'seluh)

These bell-shaped animals are given this name because of the little vortex, or whirlpool, they create when they move their long, thin cilia. They can be found in fresh water, attached to a stick or rock, where they feed on bacteria. Whenever there's trouble, their stalks contract, and they fold in their cilia. If necessary, they can break away from their stalk and swim to another spot.

Species   *V. campanula*

These greenish-colored animals are shaped like inverted bells.

PHYLUM

MESOZOA (me-zuh-'zow-uh)

("intermediate animals")

Somewhere early in the history of animals, a theory goes, a few one-celled animals came together to form a colony that could hunt as a group for food and share it equally. From this collection of single-celled Protozoa may have come the first multicellular animal. (Another theory is that the offspring of one dividing animal never quite separated from the parent, and the original one-celled individual became many-celled.) It is believed that the Mesozoa arose from such a case.

The first multicellular creature had three advantages over its one-celled friends. First, multicellular animals could grow larger and bigger because each cell was able to get the oxygen it needed, since it was either already exposed to the water or could receive oxygen through pores in the animal. Single-celled animals could only grow so large before they needed more oxygen than they could absorb. Second, the larger, multicellular creatures had more support than their one-celled neighbors because the membranes around each cell gave them that. For example, whipped cream has a greater standing power (it won't ooze off a flat table like unwhipped cream) because of the air bubbles (cells, if you wish) that hold it up. Third, with a number of cells making up the animal, each cell can share in the work of finding prey and defending the individual. In other words, each cell can do one of the jobs that parts of one cell used to do. This is how the rest of the animal kingdom arose.

The Mosozoans were the product of that development into many-celled individuals, and they may at one time have been the link (hence the name) between the primitive one-celled animals and the higher multicellular animals of today.

Mesozoans are not usually studied by the beginning biology student because these minute, wormlike animals are parasites only to marine invertebrates.

PHYLUM

PORIFERA (poh-'rif-eruh)

("pore-bearers")

Porifera, the sponges, arose some 600 million years ago from colonial Protozoa independently of other animals. Rather than heading down the path of evolutionary advancement, they never changed from their inactive (sessile) life. This is one of the reasons why they are mentioned in the scheme of taxonomy.

The sponge is no more than a living filter that attaches itself to a permanent structure like a rock. It takes in water filled with microscopic plants and animals through pores piercing its body and sends them through a larger central cavity leading to the outside. The current is caused by flagella-equipped cells lining the inner wall of the animal.

Sponges have no organs, no mouth, and no digestive

system. However, the cells that make up the body have a definite place, and groups of cells have specialized jobs. This is what is known as a cellular level of organization.

The simplest sponges are nothing more than a porous tube open at one end. More complex sponges have this general design, but the pores extend into canals.

Most sponges live in the ocean, grouped with other sponges as a colony. (There is one family that lives in fresh water.) Many reproduce by budding, dropping off a section of themselves to grow elsewhere, but there are others that reproduce sexually.

Because these animals vary so much in shape, size, color, and texture, taxonomists group sponges according to the materials in their skeletons. The support for these animals is in the form of tiny crystalline spicules that can be made either of lime or of silicon and have various shapes.

Class   CALCAREA (kal-'karee-uh)
(from the Latin *calcarius*, lime)

All of the individuals in this class live in the shallow waters of the ocean. They are simple in structure and have a skeleton made up of one- to four-rayed lime spicules that hold the body upright.

Order   HOMOCOELA (ho-mo-'seeluh) (same cavity)

This order includes some 50 species, all of which are the simplest of sponges. The body wall is thin and the wall of the inside cavity is lined with flagella-bearing cells.

FAMILY   LEUCOSOLENIIDAE (look-uh-so-'leenuh-dee)

Genus   *Leucosolenia* (lookuhsow-'leen-eeuh) (white pipe)

The simplest of the sponges, these animals grow in branching colonies attached to rocks near the shore. Each branch is nothing more than a perforated cup with a large opening, called an exhalant pore, which spews out water from the animal.

Class HEXACTINELLIDA (hek-saktuh-'neluh-duh)
(six ray)

These animals are called glass sponges because their spicules are made of silica, a component of window glass. They are given their class name because of the shapes of the spicules, all of which have six (or multiples of six) rays coming from them.

Hexactinellida live in the deep sea and their bodies often look tubular or basket-shaped. In the Venus's flower basket, one of the more well-known members, the spicules form a continuous skeleton around the animal, which seems to give the impression of spun glass.

Class DEMOSPONGIAE (deemuh-'spahn-jee-uh)
(people sponge)

Most of the sponges that you see are in this class. The most famous of them all are the popular bath sponges (though nowadays most of the sponges you see by the kitchen sink are only artificial imitations of the real animal). Demospongiae are usually quite massive and very brightly colored. They also have a very complicated canal system to pass the water through the animal and to make sure that all of the cells are fed. Their skeleton may consist of silica, or it may just have spongin (which is similar to collagen, an ingredient of gelatin), or both.

Order KERATOSA (keruh-'towsuh)

These are the commercial sponges. Occurring only in tropical and subtropical seas, the sponges (once found in the household) look very little like the sponges that sponge fishermen pull up from the sea. Once these animals are put aboard a small sponge boat, they are cleaned. The spongin

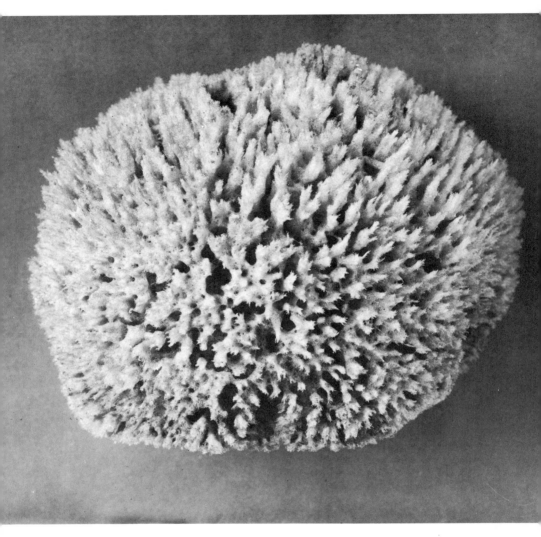

This sheepswool sponge is a member of the class Demospongiae.
(NATIONAL OCEANIC AND ATMOSPHERIC ADMINISTRATION)

skeleton is taken out, they are squeezed and rinsed, and finally they are hung up to dry.

Genus *Spongia* ('spuhn-jeeuh)

Found in the Mediterranean, these are one of the three commercial sponges.

Species *Spongia officinalis mollissima*

The best commercial sponge.

Flowers and Floating Jellies

3

PHYLUM

COELENTERATA (seh-lentuh-'rayd-uh)

(hollow-guts)

Perhaps you've walked along the beach after a heavy storm and have come across a stranded jellyfish lying on the sand. Or maybe you've bought a pretty piece of coral in a store. You probably didn't know that what you saw on the beach and what you bought in the store were related. Both are members of this phylum.

The main reason they are similar is because of their body form. Suppose you were given a tied, round balloon that was partially filled with water and were asked to poke your fist into the top of the balloon, thus creating a deep pit or cavity with your hand. What you would see would be the general form of these animals. The cavity you created would be the hollow gut, lined with cells that digest the food; the water surrounding the pit and within the balloon would be the body fluids of the animal. The rest of the balloon, surrounding both the water and the pit, would be the outside body of the animal. It's that simple. And if you were to pinch and pull the wall of the balloon around the outside of the cavity, you would have the tentacles that catch the food and put it into the gut. You would have created a model of a Coelenterata.

Most of these animals have stinging capsules on their tentacles, called *nematocysts* ('nem-at-uh-sists), that sting and paralyze their prey. In some textbooks, the phylum Coelenterata has another name, Cnidaria, which simply means that these animals possess nematocysts.

Actually, coelenterates have two basic forms, but they are still very similar. One is the polyp ("many feet"); the other is the medusa (from the Gorgon Medusa of Greek mythology that had snakes coming out of her head). The polyp is an upright form, shaped like a column. Its base is attached to a hard object like a rock or a shell, and its mouthlike opening is surrounded by tentacles. The medusa, an umbrella-shaped body called a bell, is free to swim where it pleases. It has the shape of an upside-down polyp. Usually, one form or the other is taken for all or most of its life.

Class   HYDROZOA (hidruh-'zo-uh) (hydra animals)

Hydrozoans are the simplest of the coelenterates because their hollow gut is simple. In fact, the example of the balloon describes a hydrozoan quite well. Most of these animals live in shallow salt water, but a few can be found in ponds and lakes. Even though their forms are simple, their life cycles are not. Hydrozoans alternate from a polyp stage to the free-swimming medusa stage throughout their life cycles. The polyps are small—some no bigger than the head on a penny. When it is time, they bud off small medusas that reproduce sexually, fertilizing eggs that later become polyps.

The advantage of having a medusa stage, which can swim to other places where food is more plentiful, is very important in an animal's life. But no one is quite sure which of the two forms, the medusa or the polyp, came first.

Order   HYDROIDA (hi-'droi-duh)

In most animals, the polyp and the medusa stages play an equal part in their lives. Usually, the polyps live in a colony.

Hydrozoans grab their food with stinging tentacles. This is a polyp.
(MARINE BIOLOGICAL LABORATORY)

Genus *Hydra* ('hi-druh)

Hydras are the exception to the rule. They don't have a medusa stage, they live only in fresh water, and they are solitary. Other than that, they are similar to the rest of the hydrozoans.

Hydra is no larger than the thickness of two or three pennies stacked together. It has a pillarlike body with from four to twelve hollow tentacles that may be longer than the column that supports them.

You can usually find a *Hydra* attached to the stem of a plant in a pond or floating just beneath the surface.

Hydra feeds by extending its tentacles and grabbing any tiny insect or newly hatched fish that happens to come along. Because it has stinging capsules on its tentacles, the prey have little chance of escape. And once the prey is caught, the hydra's tentacles pull the food into the gut and digestion begins.

Hydra has a very primitive nerve system. But for the tiny animal it is enough. When touched, a *Hydra* contracts into a knotted ball. But if a predator won't give up, or if there is a sudden lack of food in the area, the *Hydra* moves from its spot by gliding, or chinning (using its tentacles like arms) to another place. If it has to move more quickly, it can somersault, flipping from its flat base to its tentacles and back to its base again.

Order TRACHYLINA (trakee-'linuh) (rough linen)

Unlike the hydras, these animals live most of their lives in the medusa stage. Because medusas reproduce sexually, the polyp stage is dropped almost completely in some animals.

Genus *Gonionemus* (gow-nee-uh-'neemuhs)

Some scientists think that the primitive coelenterate was a kind of medusa and not the other way around. They believe that it looked very similar to the members of this genus.

The medusa stage of a Coelenterate is free to swim where it pleases.
(NATIONAL OCEANIC AND ATMOSPHERIC ADMINISTRATION)

These animals have a simple polyp, but their medusas are very well developed. And even though they are no larger than your little finger, they can still be seen bobbing around in saltwater ponds and by the ocean shore.

Gonionemus swim by rhythmic pulsations of their bowl-shaped bells, and they look a bit like umbrellas doing frog kicks. They have an unusual way of catching their prey. When they are feeding, they swim up to the surface, turn over, and drop toward the bottom, all the while stretching out their tentacles horizontally along the rim of the bell, much like a circular rake.

Each individual is either a male or a female. Their sex organs appear as folded ribbons hanging from the inside of a bowl.

Species *G. vertens*

This animal can be found clinging to the leaves of eelgrass or swimming freely around the saltwater ponds of New England. It is only slightly less than an inch long, and has a dark, X-shaped marking in the dome.

Order SIPHONOPHORA (sifuh-'nah-fuhr-uh) (hollow float)

Siphonophora is actually a colonial mass of five different individuals that swims in the warm oceans of the world. Each individual is a modified medusa that serves as a type of organ for the colony. One individual acts as a shield for the other members; another is modified just for swimming, or as a sac, filled with gas that keeps the whole colony floating on the surface. Another acts as a mouth for the colony; a fourth lacks a mouth but is armed with long tentacles and stinging capsules to capture prey and defend the colony against attack. A fifth may only produce new offspring. In short, the entire colony acts like a superorganism, even though it is made up of separate individuals.

Genus *Physalia* (fi-'salee-uh) (bubble)

The most famous of the Siphonophora is the "Portuguese man-of-war." Perhaps you've seen one or two of these colonial animals floating by when you've gone fishing or swimming in Florida or southern Texas. What you saw was only a small part of the colony. Floating above the surface is the blue or pink gas sac, which is really a transformed medusa. The rest of the animal colony is below the surface. In fact, the tangles of tentacles in some colonies have been known to reach as long as 60 feet.

Physalia is dangerous to people because its tentacles, which can easily paralyze a large fish, can sting a swimmer and cause a great deal of pain and discomfort. The poison in its tentacles is one of the most powerful in the marine world.

These colonies are moved by the wind, but the float can be deflated so that the colony can sink below the surface.

Class   SCYPHOZOA (sifuh-'zow-uh) (cup-animals)

The Scyphozoans are the true jellyfish. They are larger and much less delicate than the hydrozoans. Most of the medusa range about 3 or 4 feet, but some grow as large as 7 feet across the bell, with tentacles as long as a nine-story building.

All of these animals are marine. Most of them float near the surface in the shallow waters of the ocean, swimming by rhythmic contractions of their bells.

The scyphozoans have their sex organs within their bodies, which is much better than having them hanging from the bell because they are less open to attack. They are often found near the hub of the bell near the mouth.

Most of the animals have eyespots that are sensitive to light, but one genus has an eye that is nearly similar to our own.

In some cases, the medusa stage of these animals reproduces right into another medusa. In others, there is a complicated life cycle between the medusa and the very small polyp stage.

Order   SEMAEOSTOMEAE (suh-meeuh-'stowmee-ee) (standard)

This order contains most of the scyphozoans. The animals have disk-shaped bells and go from the medusa to the polyp stage throughout their lifetimes. They have large mouths with four lips and large tentacles at the margin of the umbrella.

Genus   *Aurelia* (aw-'reel-yuh) (golden)

If you have seen a large jellyfish swimming in the ocean, the chances are it was *Aurelia,* the moon jelly. They are nearly colorless, except for 4 violet circles—the sex organs—near the hub of the bell. *Aurelia,* in its medusa stage, grows to about 2½ feet. A wavy edge on its bell contains many small tentacles for grabbing the tiniest food of the sea. For a coelenterate, it is very well developed. It has eyespots that are sensitive to light, organs that can tell how the animal is moving, and small pits that can detect odors.

Aurelia has a very complex life cycle. After two medusas mate, a tiny larva settles to a rocky area and grows into a polyplike individual that later buds off a very small and very young jellyfish. As the young jellyfish grow, they feed on small fish. But as they grow even larger, their diet changes to smaller prey. Eventually, the cycle starts over again.

Class   ANTHOZOA (an-thow-'zow-uh) (flower-animals)

If you looked at a coral animal or a sea anemone (windflower), you would never know that they have almost the same kind of body as the tiny *Hydra.* Biologists can point out a lot of similarities.

Because the members of the Anthozoa have no medusa form, thay have to stay pretty much where they are for the rest of their lives. They all live in salt water.

The Anthozoans are the most advanced members of the Coelenterata because biologists classify the animals in the

Phylum by how complex their hollow gut is. The anthozoan has a very complex gut compared to the rest of the classes. The body of an anthozoan is like a very thick cylinder, with a disk at the bottom that holds the animal to a solid place and an upper disk with a slit-shaped mouth in the center. Around the mouth are the tentacles. When a small prey is caught, it is brushed into the mouth and down a short tube that acts like a throat. The throat opens into the gut. The gut of an anthozoan is divided lengthwise into partitions, or rooms. The partitions act to increase the amount of surface area that the animal can use to digest its food. The partitions are also important because they carry both the animal's reproductive organs and the well-developed muscles.

Order ACTINIARIA (ak-tinee-'a-ree-uh)

Actiniaria are the true sea anemones. When people first saw these creatures attached to a rock or to the shell of some animal, with their many tentacles waving in the currents, they must have thought they were flowers.

Sea anemones really are not much different from *Hydra,* except that they are much larger—some larger than your hand—and more muscular. These solitary animals are very often beautifully colored, but their hollow tentacles are dangerous to their prey. They have stinging capsules over their tentacles, like *Hydra.*

When one of these animals is touched, a sea anemone will fold its swaying tentacles within its body and compress itself so that it looks like a stub. But it will pop out again and start feeding as if nothing had happened. Sea anemones can move, but very slowly, and only on their bottom disk.

Genus *Metridium* (muh-'tridee-uhm) (having a womb)

The tentacles on *Metridium* are so numerous and slender that they look like a group of feathers. These animals are usually found very close to shore or in shallow pools of salt water. Like most of the other anemones, *Metridium* can regenerate, that is, it can grow a part of itself again if that part is cut or bitten off. These animals grow up to 8 inches or more.

Species *M. senile*

This large anemone has a velvet-smooth body and may be about 4 inches tall and 3 inches across. Its mouth is surrounded by fine tentacles. It occurs along the Atlantic and Pacific coasts of North America.

Order MADREPORARIA (madruh-puh-'ra-ree-uh)

If there were one group of animals that were responsible for the shape of some islands, it would have to be the animals in this order. These are the stony corals, many of which build reefs, such as the Great Barrier Reef of Australia.

Reef-building corals only grow in water that is never colder than 70°F. In the Pacific, many of the islands were formed by these corals.

When you pick up a piece of coral on a beach or buy a sculptured one in a store, what you are really picking up is a massive cluster of the empty homes of thousands of coral animals. They are colonial and, for protection, they form a limey secretion around their soft bodies, which soon hardens into a compact skeleton. When the animals die, all that is left of them is their skeletons. Soon other coral animals build their homes over other vacant homes, and this is how you see them in the ocean. The bright colors of coral reefs come from the coloring of the polyps. When they die, the coloring usually disappears.

Genus *Astrangia*

You can find this animal in colonies attached to rocks near the shore. Up close, each polyp looks like a miniature sea anemone.

Astrangia feeds on small animals, such as protozoa, hydroids, and worms, which they grab with their fine tentacles.

PHYLUM

CTENOPHORA (teh-'nahfuh-ruh)

(comb-bearer)

That jellyfish you thought you saw bobbing around in the ocean beside you may not have been a jellyfish at all. It might have been a member of the Ctenophora. They do look a little similar. But they're not.

Ctenophores are commonly called comb jellies, sea walnuts, or sea gooseberries because of their small transparent bodies. You can usually find these animals swimming feebly on the surface of the sea near the shore, struggling to overcome the currents and tides that might sweep them onto the beaches.

Ctenophores swim with eight rows of ciliary combs that radiate over the surface of the animals. Some of these tiny creatures have tentacles on each side of their bodies, which have adhesive cells that stick to their prey—shrimp and small fishes. Other species have smaller threadlike fingers that help them feed on the larvae of other animals.

If you see them up close, you can sometimes see them changing colors. This has nothing to do with the changes inside their bodies, but it does have something to do with their ciliary combs. When all of their eight rows of combs beat together, they bend the light that reflects off them like a bunch of tiny prisms, and they change colors. Some species are even phosphorescent and flash their natural lights at night.

Ctenophores are a little more advanced in some ways than the Coelenterates. They have a cell layer lining the digestive cavity, actual muscle strands (rather than just muscle cells), and definite organ systems.

Comb jellies have both ovaries and testes within their bodies, which makes it easier for them to reproduce. When

Mnemiopsis, a ctenophore, is both transparent and phosphorescent.
(WOODS HOLE OCEANOGRAPHIC INSTITUTION)

they do reproduce, the larvae develop directly into adults. There are no intermediate stages.

Biologists think that, like the sponges, ctenophores were an evolutionary dead end. They never gave rise to any other group.

Class TENTACULATA (ten-tak-yuh-'lahd-uh)

These animals have tentacles that retract into sheaths and may be long and branched, small and unbranched, or present only in the younger stages.

Order LOBATA (low-'bahd-uh)

These ctenophores have an oval body and two large lobes near their mouth which probably help them feed. They may either have very short tentacles or have their tentacles in the larvae and not in the adult.

Genus *Mnemiopsis* (nee-mee-'opsis)

Mnemiopsis is an interesting little animal that catches its tiny food by using the cilia on its body to create a current of water, which whirls the food toward the tentacles. The tentacles then entangle the prey, contract, and wipe the food into the mouth. These animals are about 4 inches in length and are both transparent and phosphorescent. At night, they flash like bulbs when they are disturbed.

Species *M. leidyi*

This creature lives between New York's Long Island and the South Carolina coastline.

The Worms that Aren't

4

PHYLUM

PLATYHELMINTHES (pladee-'helmeen-thes)

(flatworms)

More than 300 years ago, taxonomists didn't quite know what to do with all the wormlike animals in the world, so they grouped them into one phylum: the *Vermes* (the Latin word for worm). Today, biologists know that the flatworms are not really very similar to other worms, such as earthworms. So they now have a phylum all their own.

Flatworms are important for many reasons. They are the first of the animals in the taxonomic tree to have bilateral symmetry. In other words, if you slice these worms lengthwise, down the middle, each side will look the same. Flatworms are, as the name tells us, flat and ribbon thin.

Most of the flatworms are similar to the lower animals. They have a digestive cavity that is only a branched sac, and a mouth that is both for eating and for getting rid of wastes. They also have both male and female reproductive organs in their thin bodies.

On the other hand, they have actual muscle bands for movement. They have a definite head, which surrounds a tiny "brain." And they are the first animals to have their body systems controlled by organs.

Unfortunately, though, most of the flatworms are parasites, and quite a few are the parasites of people.

Class   TURBELLARIA (tuhr-buh-'lar-eeuh) (to stir)

Most of the turbellarians are not parasites, and their life cycles are simple. In any pond, or under any rock you're likely to easily find at least a dozen of them. These are the ciliated flatworms, which means that a part of their soft bodies is covered with tiny cilia (usually on their bottoms), which help them to move about.

The turbellarians range in size from a pinhead to a few inches. When they finish feeding on the small animals around them, the food goes into their intestine, to be broken down for nourishment.

Order   TRICLADIDA (tri-'klad-uh-duh) (three-branched)

The name Tricladida comes from the fact that these animals have an intestine that is branched into three parts: one part goes forward toward the head, the other two go backward from the middle of the body, where the mouth opens through a muscular tube called a *pharynx*. The bottom surface of these animals is covered with cilia.

Genus   *Dugesia* (doo-'jeezh-ee-uh)

Dugesia is probably one of the most popular animals shown and experimented on in any science class—the Planaria.

There is really nothing very special about the general shape of a planarian. It looks like a stubby arrow. At its pointed end are two light-sensitive eyes that appear cross-eyed. Actually, these are light-sensitive pigments that help the animal find shade. By the way, the pointed lobes of the "head" serve a very important purpose too. They direct the animal to food by touch.

Planarians, only about an inch long, live in ponds and lakes. These flatworms will try to eat anything they can catch or happen to find lying dead on the bottom. If their prey is too big, they just wrap it in mucus and suck off bits of it at their leisure. Sometimes, however, food is scarce. Then they feed on themselves.

One of the most interesting things about these animals is that they can grow back their entire body, or parts of it, if it is cut up. In one experiment, a scientist sliced the body of a planarian in half. The head grew back a tail, and the tail grew back a head!

Class TREMATODA (trem-uh-'towduh)
(pierced with holes)

The trematodes, or flukes, are parasites. Some of them live on the body of other animals, but most live inside other animals.

Trematodes don't look like much of anything up close. Because most of them spend their time feeding on the body fluids and tissues of their hosts, they have lost all of the sense organs that other animals need to find their prey. Flukes are different from their relatives, the turbellarians, because they don't have cilia around their bodies. They do have an armorlike material around themselves. Called the cuticle, it protects them from the digestive juices of their hosts.

Flukes look something like a deflated balloon. They may have more than two suckers that hold onto their host's body. One of the suckers is around the mouth. When a fluke sucks in the body fluids or tissues of its host, the food goes into a many-branched digestive tract to be used as nourishment.

The life cycles of these animals can be very complex. Sometimes, flukes have to pass through one or two minor hosts to get to their final host so that they can reproduce and make hundreds of new offspring. In fact, most of their bodies are filled with reproductive organs (each fluke is both a male and a female). Most of them are only as big as the letter O.

Order DIGENEA (di-'jeene-uh) (two hosts)

These animals live inside their hosts. Usually, they are found feeding in the intestine, but they have also been found in the lungs, bladder, and bloodstream of their hosts. Digenea have two hosts. In their lifetime they go from one host, usually a fish, to their final host, where the flukes mature, mate, and lay eggs. This order includes all of the species that are parasites of people.

FAMILY SCHISTOSOMATIDAE (shistuh-sow-'mad-uh-dee)

These are the blood flukes that bore into the skins of birds and mammals to feed and lay their eggs. They have long, slender bodies, and each animal is either a male or a female.

Genus *Schistosoma* (shistuh-'somuh)

The blood fluke is found in humans in much of Africa, the Middle East, the Far East, South America, and parts of the West Indies. Flukes have one host, the snail, that serves as their home before they enter through the skins of people who walk barefoot into the water. There are three species.

Species *S. japonicum*

This species is common in China, Japan, and the Philippines, where it is the parasite of two hosts.

When a person steps into the water of a rice paddy without any shoes (which most people do in those countries), he is really asking for trouble. Blood flukes in the water find a person's exposed skin and bore into it. They travel through a hundred different blood vessels until they get to the ones around the intestine. There they cling to the walls of the intestine with their powerful suckers, feeding on the body fluids. When the time comes, they lay their eggs, which soon become so numerous they break through the intestine wall and spill out into the cavity of the intestine.

Unlike the practices of this country, the people of the Far East use their body wastes as fertilizer. The egg-filled feces soon decompose, and the eggs get back into the water and hatch. When that happens, the tiny offspring find a particular species of snail (their first host), bore into its body, and feed on its tissues. Finally, they reproduce again, leave the snail, and find another person to bore into.

FAMILY OPISTHORCHIDAE (uhpis-thor-'kiuh-dee)

These animals have not one but two different hosts before they feed in the liver of their third and final host, a fish-eating mammal, bird, or reptile.

Genus *Clonorchis* (klow-'nor-kehs)

Species *C. sinensis*

One of the more infamous of the human parasites is the Chinese liver fluke, found in China, Japan, and Korea. The adults are only about half the size of a dime, but are more dangerous than the largest predator. Most of them are parasites of people, but they are also found in the livers of cats and dogs.

The eggs of a liver fluke are first eaten by a snail, in which they hatch and reproduce. Later, they leave the snail and burrow into the skin of a fish. Once they get that far, they travel to the muscles and form a hard shell around themselves.

When a person eats a piece of raw fish with flukes, the tiny flatworms go from the person's intestine to the liver to feed and start a new cycle. They lay their eggs. Then the eggs are carried outside the body, and life begins again. For the parasite, that is. Sometimes, there are so many liver flukes in a person's liver that he becomes very weak and dies.

Class CESTODA (se-'stowduh) (girdle)

If you had to design the perfect parasite, it probably

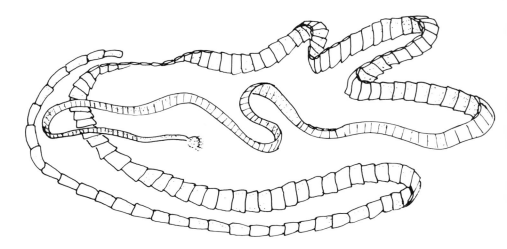

Tapeworms, members of the Platyhelminthes, are ribbon-like animals that are parasites. (DRAWING BY LAUREL STERN)

would look something like the Cestoda. At first glance, it looks like a long, flat, ribbonlike animal, with a tiny head, called a scolex. But, if you look closer, you can see that the head is not really a head at all, but a place where the animal attaches itself with suckers or hooks to the wall of the host's intestine. And the body is nothing more than a series of segments (called proglottids), each filled with reproductive organs of both sexes. Each segment can fertilize with itself or with another segment. When it is filled with eggs, it breaks off and leaves the body of the host.

Cestodes not only reproduce in large numbers, they have no mouth or digestive organs of their own. They absorb their food through their body walls, and rely on the host to find, eat, and digest their food.

Each Cestode, or tapeworm, has to be eaten to find a new host. But once they are in someone's intestine, they can grow several yards long.

Order CYCLOPHYLLIDEA (siklo-fuh-'lidee-uh)

This tapeworm has a head surrounded by four suckers. The head may even have a crown of tiny hooks to get a better hold on its host. The segments, or proglottids, break off from just below the head when they are filled with fertilized eggs.

FAMILY TAENIIDAE (tee-'ni-uh-dee)

These are very important parasites of people and other mammals.

Genus *Taenia* ('teenee-uh) (thin, stretch)

This group of animals is found in beef and pork. Taenias are eaten mostly by people, but also by cats and dogs.

Species *T. saginata*

The other name for *T. saginata* is the beef tapeworm. Today, all of the beef we eat is government inspected and without tapeworms. But in other countries where it is not inspected, a person who eats raw beef is likely to get one or more tapeworms in his intestine. Mature worms may be as long as 80 feet with at least 2,000 reproductive sections attached to their heads.

PHYLUM

NEMATODA (nemuh-'towduh)

(threadlike)

You may not know it, but at this very moment you are probably surrounded by nematodes. They are everywhere. In one acre of soil, there are some 3 billion or more free-living nematodes. In fact, a handful of dirt contains at least 100,000 individuals. Most of them are harmless to us and feed only on other nematodes and smaller microorganisms. But others are parasites of animals and plants. And there are at least fifty species that are parasites of people. You might have been a host to one at some time!

Roundworms, as they're called, are not much like earthworms, even though they may look a bit like them. Roundworms are more primitive. They do not have a complex nervous system or a complicated body structure. They resemble earthworms in that they have lean, cylinderlike bodies that are pointed at both ends. They even have a mouth at one end that sucks in food, and an anus at the other.

Most nematodes look like tiny pieces of moving thread. They are covered by a thick cuticle that protects them from digestive juices if they are parasites, and from the rough dirt, if they are free-living.

All free-living roundworms are very small. Most of them are transparent except for their colored eye spots. Each has a mouth, lips, and teeth, but does not chew its food. The free-living animals get around in the dirt by whipping their bodies like a constantly moving S. Without something solid

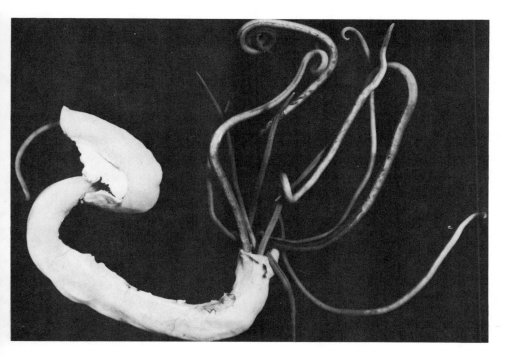

Parasitic nematodes, like these worms found in the intestine of a hog, are very harmful. (U.S. DEPARTMENT OF AGRICULTURE)

around them, they wiggle endlessly without going anywhere. But as soon as they are put into some dirt, they can disappear in an instant.

The parasitic nematodes are usually much larger, sometimes more than the length of your arm. They have no organs of touch, taste, and smell, and their life cycles are more complicated.

Both types of roundworms are either male or female.

Class   NEMATODA: The same as phylum.

Order   TRICHUROIDEA (trikee-'yuroi-dee-uh)

These are the parasites of the vertebrates. They have a mouth with no lips, and a long and narrow mouth cavity that helps to suck in and move their food. The front part of their body is narrower than the rear half.

Genus   *Trichinella* (trikuh-'neluh)

The *Trichinella* are unusual parasites. They enter the body of their first host when they are brought into the mouth with the food. The small worms mature and soon deposit as many as 10,000 young in the host's intestine. But the young don't go out with the waste. Instead, they burrow through the wall of the intestine and form a case around themselves in the host's muscles. When the second host eats the uncooked meat of the first host, the tiny worms go through the second host's intestine and into the muscles.

Species   *T. spiralis*

This is a very important animal because it causes a disease—trichinosis—in people, pigs, and rats. When uncooked pork is eaten by a person, the cases around the worms digest away. The now-active roundworms develop in the person's intestine, bore into the muscles, and again surround themselves with a casing. One or two roundworms aren't too much of a problem. The real trouble starts when nearly a billion of the young worms bore into the muscles. They can cause severe pain, fever, weakness, and even death.

Order ASCAROIDEA (as-kuh-'roidee-uh)

Here the members are the intestinal worms of vertebrates. They are usually large and have a mouth with three lips.

Genus *Ascaris* ('askuh-rehs)

Ascaris shows just how difficult it is to be a parasite. The eggs of these roundworms first leave a host with the feces. When food, with some of the eggs on it, is eaten, the eggs hatch. The very young nematodes journey through the blood to the lung, where they grow and develop some more. And when the time comes, they pierce the lung wall, go up the respiratory tract, enter the pharynx, get into the digestive tract, journey into the stomach, and finally stop in the intestine. There they mate and lay eggs.

Species *A. lumbricoides* ('luhm-bruh-koid-s)

This worm parasitizes people. The journey from the mouth to the intestine takes about ten days, but it takes more than two months for these worms to mature. The adult females are about 10 inches in length and a ¼ inch in diameter. Their bodies are milky-white or reddish-yellow. *A. lumbricoides* lays many eggs—200,000 per day or more—which go out with the rest of the waste. But if you think that their journey through your body is a harmless one, you're wrong. If these worms have passed through someone's lungs, the person can become very sick. And if too many worms get into a person's intestine, they can clog it up.

Order STRONGYLOIDEA (strahn-'jiluh-dee)

These parasites live in the intestine of their vertebrate hosts and suck on their blood. They have simple, lipless mouths.

FAMILY ANCYLOSTOMIDAE ('ankeh-low-'stahmeh-dee)

These animals live in the intestine of many meat-eaters, such as dogs, cats, tigers, lions, and wolves. They also parasitize people, pigs, and chimpanzees. The hookworms are in this family.

Genus *Necator* (neh-'kad-uhr) (killer)

Hookworms, like *Ascaris,* also have a long journey to make before they can mate. The eggs of these worms first hatch in moist soil and do no harm until they get into a host's foot. They bore through the soft skin, enter the veins, pass through the heart to the lungs, travel up the windpipe and into the throat. Then they are swallowed, and travel down past the stomach, where they finally attach themselves to the walls of the intestine.

Hookworms are only about ½ inch long when they finally reach their destination, but they do a lot of damage. They latch onto the wall of the intestine with their hooklike teeth and shoot poison into the hole they have made. This keeps the blood from clotting while they suck on it. The host loses a lot of blood and becomes very sick.

Species *N. americanus*

These animals only attack people and pigs. When people go barefoot around places where there are feces dropped by other people or by domesticated animals, they stand a good chance of getting infected. In the 1930s, some 2 million people in this country were afflicted with this parasite.

PHYLUM

NEMATOMORPHA (nemuh-tah-'morfuh)

(form of a thread)

Many years ago, people thought that if a hair from a

horse fell into a barrel of water, the barrel would be filled with "horsehair snakes" the next day. Today, biologists know that what these people saw were the adult stages of parasites that had left the bodies of insect or crab hosts, which had somehow fallen into the water.

Horsehair worms, as they are called, are strange creatures. They look like nematodes, except that they don't have a mouth. Instead, they absorb their food through their body surfaces. Some are about 12 inches long and dark colored. But most are smaller.

The only goal of a horsehair worm is to reproduce. But they go about it in such a strange way that you might wonder why they are still around today. Only the young worms, or larvae, are parasites. They live in the bodies of insects or crabs until they reach adulthood. When they are mature, they leave the host and live a free life in the water, searching for mates. But they don't live long after that. The males die immediately after they mate, and the females die as soon as they lay their eggs.

PHYLUM

ROTIFERA (row-'tif-eruh)

(wheel-bearers)

You might think that the more complex an animal is, the larger it has to be. Not so with the rotifers. They can only be seen with a microscope. In fact, some of them are even smaller than one-celled animals, such as the amoeba. Rotifers live in all kinds of environments. Most of them live in fresh water, but there are many that live in the ocean, and a few that only live in the bodies of other animals.

Rotifers feed on bacteria and Protozoa. But one way in which they catch their food is similar to one way in which vorticellas catch theirs. The head of a free-living rotifer is surrounded by cilia that beat the water and create a current (the rotation or "wheel" effect is what gives these animals their name). The current pulls in the food, and it is swept into the mouth. But, unlike the vorticella, the rotifer has a rather complex digestive system. The food travels from the mouth into a chewing stomach, where it is ground into smaller parts by the jaws. Then it goes into the digestive stomach, where it is broken down some more. Finally, it arrives in the intestine. Rotifers also swim around by means of their cilia.

One of the ways these animals have learned to survive is by making their eggs resistant to harsh elements of the environment. Even high temperatures and dried-up lakes do not destroy their thick-shelled eggs.

Prisoners of the Shell

5

PHYLUM

MOLLUSCA (muh-'luhskuh)

(soft-bodied)

Snails, slugs, clams, squids, and octopuses belong to the same phylum. But if you looked at them, you wouldn't think so because they all are different in appearance. It was about 600 million years ago that the first mollusk began its life on this earth. It looked very different from the mollusks of today. Scientists think that the original animal might have been a soft-bodied one, with a mouth at one end and an anus at the other. Today, there are at least 80,000 living species of mollusks, not to mention 35,000 fossils that have crawled or swum on this planet.

It's true that animals, such as squid and clams, look very different. But they have many things in common. For instance, all have mantles that cover their bodies and secrete shells. And all of them have well-developed digestive tracts, circulatory systems with hearts, kidneys, and something you might call brains. Most of them have definite heads and special sense organs, and each of them has a muscular foot, used for locomotion. Most of the mollusks also have a radula—a ribbon-shaped, rasping organ that slides back and forth in the mouth, scraping off particles of food.

Class AMPHINEURA (amfi-'nuruh)

Probably one of the simplest mollusks, the fossils of these animals are believed to be 600 million years old. Most of them have an oval-shaped body, with a mouth at one end and an anus at the other. They are also bilaterally symmetrical (each side of the body looks the same), which the earliest mollusks probably were. But the head is not very well developed and they do not have any eyes. They live on the bottom of the ocean, near the shore.

Order POLYPLACOPHORA (pahlee-pla-'kahfuhr-uh)

The chitons, as they're called, are the simplest of the living mollusks, but they are not the most primitive. Biologists think that these animals may have looked different millions of years ago and may have changed since. They have an oval body that may be smaller than your thumb, although there are giant chitons that are a foot or more in length. On their arched backs are a series of 8 plates that help protect them from their enemies.

Chitons feed on algae, which they scrape off rocks with their mouths. They do little else. Most of the time they stay in a definite spot, holding onto a rock with a long, flat foot, which acts like a suction cup. When they do leave their home to feed, they always come back, returning to the exact spot from which they left. This sense of security is so strong in some species, that they live their entire lives in the depressions formed by past generations of chitons. They live in the sea, at any depth and in any temperature of water.

Class GASTROPODA (ga-'strah-puh-duh) (belly foot)

Snails and their relatives are rather puzzling creatures. Most of them have coiled shells (although there are some that don't have any shells at all) that spiral to the right. Most of them have a distinct head, with well-developed sense organs, but scientists don't know what their ancestors looked

like. Most of the gastropods live in salt water, but there are a
few that live on land, and even some that live in freshwater
lakes and ponds. Why did they decide to leave the ocean? No
one has the real answer; they can only guess.

Gastropods creep along on their belly surfaces, secreting
a mucus that helps to smooth the ride.

Order PROSOBRANCHIA (prah-suh-'brankee-ah)

This order contains most of the gastropods. Many of
them are marine and have coiled shells. The sexes are
separate.

FAMILY ACMAEIDAE (ak-'meeuh-dee)

You can't see much of a limpet, hiding under its conelike shell, because it rarely leaves its spot on a rock in the
ocean. In fact, its suction grip on a rock is so strong that, if
you could manage to pull it off, you could see the ring it
made on the rock with its shell.

FAMILY HALIOTIDAE (halee-'oduh-dee)

The abalones are marine gastropods with flat spiral
shells that have large openings. They are edible and deli-
cious, and their shells are made into jewelry, especially
buttons.

FAMILY LITTORINIDAE (lid-uh-'rinuh-dee)

Periwinkles live in salt or fresh water. They have pretty
shells that are both conical and spiral. The animals themselves have eyes at the base of their tentacles.

Genus *Littorina* (lid-uh-'rinuh)

Littorina, the small periwinkles, are interesting animals
to biologists. They are found in large clusters throughout the
world, inside crevices and cracks of rocks. They eat plants
and lichen. One of the reasons some snails left the sea can be
seen by the way in which these animals distribute themselves

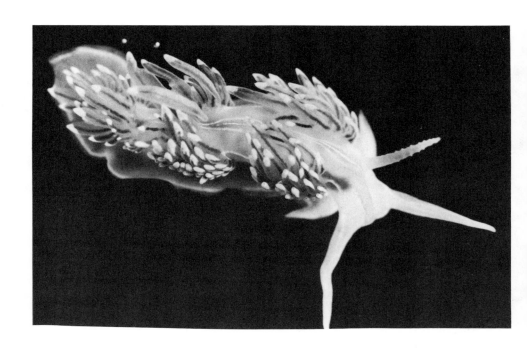

Some nudibranchs adopt the nematocysts of the prey they eat for their own defense. (MARINE BIOLOGICAL LABORATORY)

by the shore. Each particular species is only adapted to so much water or air exposure to live. For example, there is one species that is covered most of the time with water and would die if exposed to air. Yet another species in the same genus lives high on the rocks and only gets spray from the surf. It would die if submerged in water.

Order   NUDIBRANCHIA (nu-duh-'brankee-uh) (naked gills)

Many millions of years ago, certain sea snails gradually lost all of their shells, possibly because their large homes became too cumbersome. Today, these sea slugs are some of the most beautiful animals in the ocean.

Many sea slugs live mostly among seaweed and under rocks near the shore, where they feed on hydroids and snail eggs. They don't have true gills like other gastropods, but they do have modified gills that are exposed to water. These naked gills, called *cerata,* look like tiny flowers on some animals. Sea slugs have reproductive organs of both sexes.

FAMILY   AEOLIDIDAE (ee-uh-'liduh-dee)

When one of these sea slugs eats a hydroid, something very interesting happens. It digests everything except the hydroid's nematocysts, or stinging capsules. The sea slugs have groups of fingerlike projections on their backs, which are really part of their intestines. When they eat a hydroid, the nematocysts travel to the tips of these "fingers" and stay there. If a predator tries to take a nip at these animals and manages to bite off a "finger" or two, it gets a very unpleasant surprise.

Order   PULMONATA (pulmuh-'nah-duh)

While many of the gastropods stayed in the ocean, a few moved out of the sea and onto the land. Some moved into fresh water. But when they made their move out of the ocean, they lost their gills. Evolution was kind to them, though, and a cavity developed in their mantle, which served as a lung.

Freshwater and land snails have one or two pairs of tentacles on their heads, which they use to sense the environment. The shell, if they have one, is shaped like a simple coil.

In some ways, these snails are more modern than the ocean snails. The latter cast their eggs outside their bodies to be fertilized by the males. Freshwater and land snails fertilize the eggs while they're still inside the female. The tiny snails are born with shells already on their backs. The shells become bigger as the young grow.

FAMILY   HELICIDAE (heh-'liseh-dee)

These are terrestrial snails that have shells with flat, conelike spires. The animals have two pairs of tentacles, which can retract into their bodies like a submarine periscope if danger approaches. Another interesting thing about these snails is that they have their eyes at the tips of their rear tentacles. If another animal tries to attack them, the snails pull their eyes inside their heads. But even if a predator does manage to eat one of the tentacle eyes, the snails can grow new ones.

Genus   *Helix* ('hee-liks)

Helix are some of the largest land snails. They feed on the leaves and fruits of trees during the summer months and hibernate during the colder months. Most of them can be eaten by people.

Species   *H. pomatia*

Almost anyone who has ever eaten in a French restaurant is familiar with this snail. It is the *escargot,* the French word for snail. One of the largest of the edible snails, it has a thick, round shell that is pale yellow.

Class   SCAPHOPODA (skuh-'fah-puh-duh)

If you walk along a beach in Florida, you're likely to find a shell that looks like the tusk of a tiny elephant. This is the tusk shell of a marine animal that buries itself in the mud or sand and feeds on the tiny animals floating by. Unfortunately, not much is known about them.

Class PELECYPODA (peluh-'sip-uh-duh) (hatchet foot)

Another name for this animal is bivalve. This mollusk has a two-part shell, hinged at one side. It is opened and shut with the bivalve's muscles. Pelecypoda include some of the most familiar members of the mollusks: clams, oysters, scallops, cockles, and mussels. Many of the animals have a foot shaped like a hatchet.

Most of the bivalves stay in one place nearly all of their lives, except when they are floating around in the water as larvae. They feed by sifting their food across their gills like a strainer. Because of their nonmoving lives, their heads have merged with the rest of their bodies. Some of their sense organs are simpler than those of most other mollusks. There are bivalves in the ocean and in ponds and lakes, but none of them lives on land.

Order FILIBRANCHIA (filuh-'brank-ee-uh)

These marine animals have two rows of long, featherlike gills that hang down from their mantles like socks hung up to dry. Most of these animals secrete thin but very tough threads (called *byssus threads)* from their feet, which help them anchor their shells to solid places like rocks.

FAMILY MYTILIDAE (mi-'tiluh-dee)

A very ancient group, mussels live in every sea at varying depths. Mussels are familiar to anyone who has waded in tidal pools. Many of the species vary in shape, but they all have shells that are equal to each other and long. Usually, they are wedge-shaped or oval. They also may be smooth or ribbed. The foot of the mussel is shaped like a cylinder and can be extended to attach itself with the byssus threads.

FAMILY   PECTINIDAE (pek-'tinuh-dee)

Most of the bivalves rarely, if ever, move from one spot on the sand. The members of the scallop family are the exception to the rule. When scallops are young, they attach themselves with their byssus threads to something hard. But when many of the species grow older, they break free of their attachments. Unlike most of the bivalves, scallops have the ability to swim short distances by clapping their two valves together very rapidly. This pushes them through the water and helps them to escape predators, such as starfish.

Many scallops have beautiful shells. Each valve has a wing near the attachment to the other valve. And the shell itself has ribs that radiate outward from the attachment.

Scallop shells were important to early civilizations. They were used as utensils by primitive man. In Greek mythology, Aphrodite (Venus) was said to have arisen fully mature from a scallop. And during the Renaissance of Europe (14th to the 17th century), scallops were featured in both art and architecture.

The large muscle, called the adductor muscle, can be eaten and is the "scallop" served in restaurants.

FAMILY   OSTREIDAE (ah-'stree-uh-dee)

At one time, oysters were more mobile than they are today. But evolution slowly changed them to a life of non-movement. Their valves are unequal and very irregular, and almost every individual oyster has a different shell. Oysters live in shallow inshore waters of the ocean on most continents.

Nearly everyone knows that we get most of our pearls from these abundant animals. But the most valuable pearls are the inner layers of the shells, wrapped thickly over grains of sand or tiny animals on tropical oysters.

Order   EULAMELLIBRANCHIA (yu-luh-'meluh-brank-ee-uh)

The name simply means that the two gills of these animals have featherlike leaflets that are connected into two comblike structures.

This animal lives in both fresh and salt water. It has a large foot and two adductor muscles that keep its shells closed for protection against predators. It also has a tubelike organ connected to its mouth. Called a siphon, it can suck in water and draw it over the gills. This is very important to those animals that bury themselves deeply under the sand and mud and need a long reach to get water.

FAMILY TRIDACNIDAE (tri-'daknuh-dee)

These species include the giant marine clams of the coral reefs.

Genus *Tridacna* (tri-'daknuh) (eaten at three bites)

These bivalves are so big that you could probably take a bath in one of their valves. And they are so heavy that it takes several strong men to lift one. But, despite what is shown in movies and on TV, *Tridacna* are harmless. Their food is the smallest of sea creatures, plankton. *Tridacna* live, hinge down, in holes that they bore themselves in beds of coral.

FAMILY VENERIDAE (veh-'neruh-dee)

These thick-shelled clams bury themselves in the sand or mud of the ocean.

Genus *Mercenaria* (muhrs-n-'a-ree-uh)

Species *M. mercenaria*

Quahogs, or cherrystone clams, are native to the Atlantic coast of North America. They burrow straight down into the sand and stick their siphons, or necks, into the water to feed. Both are edible.

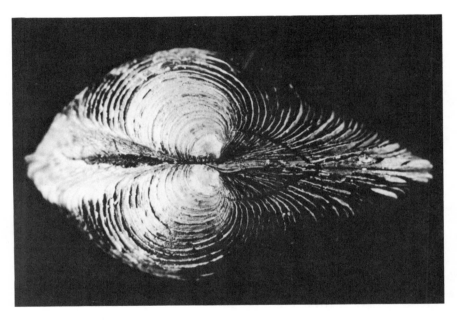

The quahog, M. mercenaria, is a bivalve that feeds by sticking its neck into the water. (MARINE BIOLOGICAL LABORATORY)

FAMILY   MYACIDAE (mi-'asuh-dee)

These animals live in salt water and burrow into the sand. Their shells are dingy gray.

Genus   *Mya* ('mi-uh)

Species   *M. arenaria* (aruh-'na-reuh)

We've all eaten these clams at one time or another. We've had them steamed, in clam chowder, or in a clam dip. They are the long-necks—the soft-shell clams. When they have buried themselves in the sand, they stretch their long necks into the water and feed like the quahogs.

FAMILY   SOLENIDAE (so-'lenuh-dee)

The shells of this family are thin and narrow, growing to 3 or 4 inches in length. Razor clams are included in this group.

The solenida has a large foot that it uses to rapidly bury itself deep within the sand. The foothold that it has is sometimes so strong that if you pulled on the animal, you would probably break it in two before you got all of it out of the sand.

Class   CEPHALOPODA (sefuh-'lah-puh-duh) (head-footed)

Cephalopods, which include the squids, octopuses, and their relatives, are some of the most modern animals without backbones. They have the most highly developed nervous systems in the animal kingdom, excluding the vertebrates, and many people would not be wrong to call them intelligent. In fact, scientists have found that they can actually learn from their mistakes. It's also surprising to find that they all have vertebratelike eyes that can actually focus on an object, much as our own eyes can.

These animals may look unusual, but they are not much different from bivalves and snails. The cephalopod has a mantle that, in the other mollusks like the snails, secretes a shell. It also has a foot. But the foot is divided into a number of arms that are wrapped around its head. Cephalopods move around the ocean by jet propulsion. A funnel, which also serves to bring water to the gills, jets out water in one direction while the animal moves forward in the other. If chased by a predator, the cephalopod creates an inky screen that clouds the water.

Order   DIBRANCHIA (di-'bran-keeuh)

This mollusk has a single pair of gills and a very small shell, which is surrounded by its body. It also has 10 tentacles. One pair, longer than the others, has suckers near the end; the other four pairs are shorter and have suckers along their entire lengths.

FAMILY   LOLIGINIDAE (lah-luh-'jin-uh-dee)

The squids in this family have long bodies with fins near the ends of them. Their eyes are very well developed.

Genus   *Loligo* (lo-'li-go) (cuttlefish)

These squids are common in the offshore waters of the Atlantic Ocean. They have torpedo-shaped bodies that may be as long as a foot, and they catch small fish, crustaceans, and other squids.

Species   *L. pealii*

One of the most common squids along the eastern coast of North America, *L. pealii* lives in deep water during the winter. Early in May it enters the shallow waters in large groups, called schools, to lay its eggs. These squids have very large nerves that have been closely studied. Many of the facts about our own nervous system have come from experiments on the squid's nerves.

Order OCTOPODA (ahk-'tah-puh-duh) (eight feet)

The members of this order have shortened, rounded bodies and no shells. They also have eight arms.

Octopods, or octopuses and their relatives are not the aggressive giants Hollywood has made them out to be. They are very shy, and they shun any person's attempt to get close to them. Octopods vary in size. A few species are only 1½ inches long. And even the bodies of the largest octopods are only about 18 inches in diameter. But their arm spread may be more than 32 feet.

Octopods are divided according to where they live in the ocean.

FAMILY OCTOPODIDAE (ahk-tuh-'pahduh-dee)

These octopods live in the shallow seas. They have very large heads.

Genus *Octopus* ('ahk-tuh-poos)

Octopuses (or octopi) move by crawling on the bottom with their eight arms. They feed mainly on crabs and lobsters, which they bite with their horny-beaked mouths. Like the snails, they also have radula for drilling into the shells of their prey.

When an octopus is alarmed, it shoots backward, meanwhile ejecting ink from its body as a smoke screen. In some species, the ink also paralyzes the sense organs of the attacker.

Species *O. vulgaris* (vahl-'gar-is) (common)

The common octopus lives in holes along the rocky bottom of warm seas. It is a shy but intelligent animal. *O. vulgaris* has a sacklike body with large, complex eyes, and arms with two rows of suckers. The males and females of the species mate in the winter. The female hangs her eggs, like beads, on the roof of her home, never letting them out of her sight for eight weeks, when they finally hatch.

Octopuses are shy mollusks that feed on crabs and lobsters. (STATE OF FLORIDA DEPT. OF COMMERCE)

Sections
and
Joints

6

PHYLUM

ANNELIDA (uh-'nel-uh-duh)

About 550 million years ago, a simple worm became an annelid. Today, there are some 8,500 different kinds of earthworms, bristle worms, and leeches that live in nearly every kind of environment, including other animals.

If you take a close look at the body of a worm, you will see that it seems to be divided into a series of rings or ringlike grooves. Actually, each ring is just the outer part of a partition inside the animal. Annelida have segmented bodies; each part of their body is really a tiny room—something like the cars that make up a train.

Scientists believe that segmentation might have come from the primitive worm's need to burrow. Having a segmented body means that it could stretch one fluid-filled chamber, while at the same time shortening another by two or three segments. This gave it far more thrust, or pushing power, than an unsegmented worm.

Although each segment of this soft-bodied animal has its own muscles, nerves, blood vessels, and digestive tract, they are connected by a larger gut and a set of nerves that run the length of the worm's body. The gut leads to an anus.

While the middle segments of the annelids are usually very similar to one another, the ones near the mouth are not. In many of the animals, they are specialized, or modified, for feeding and for breathing. On the outside of each segment there is a group of bristles, which (depending on the kind of worm) are used for swimming, breathing, or feeding.

Class   POLYCHAETA (pahlee-'keed-uh) (many bristles)

Most of the annelids belong to this class of marine worms. *Polychaetes*, or bristle worms, have segments that are easy to see and well-defined heads with eyes and antennae. Each segment behind the head has a group of paddles, supported by bristles, that help the animal breath and move. This is important because many of the polychaetes are active animal-eaters and must swim or crawl to reach their food. A few, however, live most or all of their lives in tubes, which they build on the ocean bottom.

Polychaetes are very numerous on the ocean floor. Thousands of them may live in an area the size of a desk. They are also important to the food chain of the sea, and are eaten by hydroids, flatworms, and other animals.

The sexes are separate in many species.

Order   ERRANTIA (eh-'ranch-eeuh)

These animals crawl, swim, or burrow. And sometimes they do all three. A few of them live in tubes, but they rarely stay in them their entire lifetimes. Most of them are active hunters, with well-developed sense organs. But these annelids are more primitive than other worms. Their body segments are all the same, except for their mouths and anus ends, which look different. Their heads are equipped with extendable tubes, or pharynxes, armed with jaws.

FAMILY   NEREIDAE (neh-'reeuh-dee)

The members of this family have a jagged look to their bodies, caused by the paddles that jut out from their segments. In fact, most people call them "rag worms" for just that reason. Rag worms, which are used as bait by fishermen, burrow mostly in sand or mud, although a few live under stones on the shore. Each has a bulge in front of its first segment with two short antennae and four eyes on it. The animal also has jaws that are studded with teeth.

Order SEDENTARIA (sed-n-'tar-eeuh)

All of these worms are perfectly adapted for their quiet, nonmobile life in the soft bottoms of the sea. Many of them build tubes around themselves and live their entire lives in them. Others burrow without tubes. The head of this animal may be small, with few or no paddles. Or it may be modified, with huge, feathery gills projecting from it. Its pharynx cannot be extended and it has no jaws.

FAMILY CHAETOPTERIDAE (kee-'tahp-tuhruh-dee)

Usually, these annelids live in vertical tubes that project slightly into the water. There, they feed on the tiny animals that are swept into their homes. The food gets trapped in a mucus bag beside their bodies which is secreted by their paddles. They eat by swallowing the bag.

Genus *Chaetopterus* (kee-'tahp-tuhr-uhs)

Chaetopterus live in U-shaped tubes under the sand or mud, very close to the low-tide mark of a shore. The worms may be as long as an adult's hand, and nearly every segment is different in shape. The worms spend all of their time pulling in currents of water through their tubes with their paddles.

FAMILY SABELLIDAE (suh-'beleh-dee)

These worms live in tubes and have feathered gills, or breathing organs, that wave in the water.

Genus *Sabella* (suh-'beluh)

Sabella, or feather-duster worms live in tubes 15 inches long. Most of the time their two tufts of long, plumelike gills stick into the water. If they are touched, they will withdraw into their tubes.

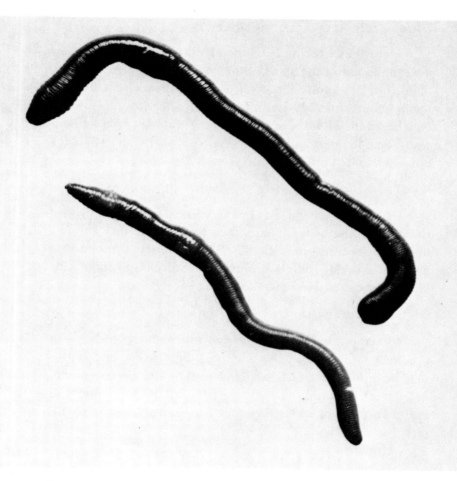

Earthworms have both male and female sex organs in their bodies.
(U.S. DEPT. OF AGRICULTURE)

Class OLIGOCHAETA (ahleh-go-'keed-uh) (few bristles)

Land worms (earthworms), freshwater worms, and a very few marine worms, belong to this group. They are different from the polychaetes in several ways. Their bodies have no paddles and very few bristles. They also have small heads. Since most of them plow through the ground, any projections on their heads would slow them down or become damaged. Oligochaets also differ from polychaetes, because each oligochaet (earthworm) has the organs of both sexes. Unlike the marine worms, they don't go through a larval stage.

Earthworms are larger than the freshwater species, which may only be visible under a microscope. Some earthworms are large; one Australian species reaches over 10 feet (about 3 meters).

Nearly every earthworm has a section, or saddle, around its body that is larger and smoother than the rest. This is very important when the worm has to lay its eggs. The saddle is near the reproductive segments. When the eggs are ready to be laid, the saddle produces a mucus belt that helps get the eggs and sperm together and makes a cocoon for the growing embryos.

These worms have no lungs or gills. They must get their oxygen through their body surfaces. And because water is needed for this to happen, they must stay moist at all times.

They are classified by their sex organs.

Order PLESIOPORA ('pleesuh-puhruh)

These annelids are small worms that have sperm ducts open to the air in a segment behind the one containing the testes.

FAMILY TUBIFICIDAE (toobuh-'fisuh-dee)

These slender worms live in tubes in lakes, ponds, and river beds. They have four bundles of bristles on each of their segments.

Genus   *Tubifex* ('toobuh-feks)

Tubifex are no longer than 1 inch. They feed on the decaying material of animals on the bottom mud of deep lakes and polluted streams where there is very little oxygen. Tubifex breathe and feed by holding onto their tubes with their heads and waving their tails in the water.

Species   *T. tubifex*

This is a red-colored species, sold as food for aquarium fish.

Order   OPISTHOPORA (uh-'pisthuh-puhruh)

These large earthworms have many segments and reproduce sexually. Their sperm duct opening is usually several segments behind the segment with the testes.

FAMILY   LUMBRICIDAE (luhm-'brisuh-dee)

The members include the common earthworms of Eurasia and North America.

Genus   *Lumbricus* ('luhm-bruh-kuhs)

Species   *L. terrestris*

"Night crawlers" are usually the ones teachers show in class. The animal grows to about 1 foot (30 centimeters) long, and has over 100 segments and a flattened tail. These worms pull leaves and sticks into their burrows and feed on the decaying matter.

Class   HIRUDINEA (hiruh-'dineeuh)

Most leeches are found in fresh water and on land, but there are also a few species that live in the ocean. Scientists believe that these animals may have evolved from the ancestors of the oligochaets because they are segmented (in fact, all of them have only 33 segments). They are the most specialized of the annelids. Unlike earthworms, leeches have bodies that are flat and that come nearly to a point at both ends. Their first and last segments are modified as suckers, the last being the larger one.

While a few of the leeches are predators that capture and swallow their prey whole, most of them are bloodsuckers. They attach themselves to the softest part of the skin with their rear sucker. Then they slice the skin with sharp, knifelike jaws, or dissolve the skin with their own juices. Leeches usually feed on the free-flowing blood until they nearly burst. Then they stop for a while, detach themselves, and look for another victim.

Order GNATHOBDELLIDA (naythahb-'deleh-duh)

These leeches usually have jaws and live in fresh water and on land.

FAMILY HIRUDINIDAE (hiruh-'dinuh-dee)

The members of this family have three-toothed jaws and five pairs of eyes, which don't focus like ours. They are the bloodsuckers of frogs, fish, horses, cattle, and people.

Genus *Hirudo* (heh-'roo-do)

Species *H. medicinalis*

This greenish-colored leech, with long, red stripes, lives in ponds. When it is fully grown, it may expand 6 to 12 inches (15 to 30 cm). It is called the "medicinal leech" because it was once used to suck out the "bad blood" of sick patients—a process called leeching. Today it is still used to remove the color from a black eye.

PHYLUM

ARTHROPODA (ahr-'thrahp-uh-duh)

(jointed feet)

Eighty percent of all the animal species on earth belong to this phylum. We've heard about or seen most of them: lobsters, crabs, mites, barnacles, millipeds, spiders, insects, and a host of other lesser-known animals. They are found everywhere, including the deepest oceans and the highest mountains. A million species have been discovered by biologists and another million are probably waiting to be found. If numbers mean success in nature, arthropods have been very successful.

Arthropods evolved from the same ancestor the annelids did. In fact, both groups have segmented bodies. But arthropods were able to adapt more efficiently to the environment by changing their bodies. The light cuticle around the worms is harder and thicker in the arthropods. It became their support, or *exoskeleton*. While the worms moved about with paddles, the arthropods evolved legs that were divided into movable joints for faster and more agile movement. Even their muscles became more efficient. While the worms had segments that were more or less similar, the arthropods fused and modified their segments into important sections of their bodies.

Today's arthropods have not only fairly efficient breathing systems (the first phylum to evolve one up to now), but they also have highly developed nervous systems, with complicated sense organs, such as antennae and eyes.

Unfortunately, however, these animals are the prisoners of their own design. When they grow to a certain size, they must molt, or pop out of their old exoskeleton, and grow a new one.

What follows is just a sample of the enormous number of members in this group.

Class CRUSTACEA (kruh-'stāsh-uh) (with a crust or shell)

Crustaceans, which include the crayfish, lobsters, crabs, shrimps, and barnacles, have bodies that are usually divided into three sections—actually a bunch of segments fused together. The head is made up of five segments. Attached to the head are two pairs of feelers, one pair of jaws, and two pairs of mouth parts. The thorax, or breastplate, is next on the body and bears the walking legs. The final part of the body is called the abdomen, usually nothing more than the tail on a large number of the animals. Many times, however, even the head and the thorax are fused together. Lobsters and crabs are good examples of this.

Most crustaceans live in the water and breathe with gills, but a very few live on land.

Order THORACICA (thuh-'ras-ehkuh)

Years ago, barnacles used to be grouped with mollusks because they looked just like them. But it was not until someone looked closely at the larvae of these animals that the truth was known.

A freely drifting larva first attaches its head to a hard support, like a rock or a boat's hull. Upside-down, it stops feeding, dissolves its eyes and its abdomen, lessens its paired legs to four or six feathery feet, and secretes a lime shell around itself, with a movable door that can be opened and closed. Finally, it opens up the door for business, sweeping in with its feet whatever passes by.

FAMILY BALANIDAE (buh-'lanuh-dee)

This nonmoving group, which includes acorn barnacles, is highly evolved.

Genus *Balanus* ('bal-uh-nuhs)

Acorn barnacles are found by the shore and in deeper water.

Species   *B. balanoides*

You're likely to find these common, thick-shelled rock barnacles near the shores of the Atlantic and Pacific oceans. They are also the ones you usually find on the hulls of boats.

Order   EUPHAUSIACEA (yoo-fawzee-'asheeuh) (shining light)

These are the "krill" that whales especially like to eat. Like many whales, they are filter-feeders themselves, and are important in the food chain. Unlike the shrimps, the legs on these animals are not designed for grabbing or biting, since the food they eat is too small to handle.

Order   DECAPODA (deh-'kap-uh-duh) (ten feet)

By far the largest and most well-known of the crustaceans, the decapods consist of about 8,000 species, including lobsters, crabs, shrimps, and crayfish.

Decapods can usually be easily spotted. They have plates of exoskeletons that cover nearly all of their backs except for their tails; five pairs of walking legs (the first pair usually much larger, with thick pincer claws); and are either flat, top and bottom like crabs, or flat, side to side, like lobsters.

When they are not actively hunting for scraps of food, the females produce hundreds of eggs, which usually hatch as free-swimming larvae.

FAMILY   PENEIDAE (peh-'neeuh-dee)

In the warmer waters of the ocean you may find these animals swimming in large schools, looking for weaker crustaceans, worms, and small fish to feed on. Prawns, which resemble shrimps in many ways, except size (prawns are usually bigger), have long bodies that are slightly flat from side to side. Usually, they swim forward, using the legs on their abdomens, which are adapted for paddling through the water. But, they may dart backwards, propelled by their fan-like tails. They make an excellent meal for most people in England and Europe.

FAMILY HOMARIDAE (ho-'maruh-dee)

Like most lobsters, these hard-shelled, large-clawed animals will eat nearly anything, including themselves. They are cannibalistic. Lobsters have large, well-developed tails, which help them move away from their enemies in a hurry, and each of their thinner rear legs ends with a claw. For added defense, their skeletons are equipped with thornlike spines, which they use in case of attack. Like most of their close relatives, these animals split their shells along the back when they molt, and ease out of their tight-fitting skeleton. Although a leg may be lost in the process, it eventually grows back. For several days after they leave their first shells, they are very soft and easy targets for predators. So they often hide somewhere, extracting lime from their old shells and from the water, until their new skin hardens.

Genus *Homarus* ('hawm-uh-ruhs)

These are common lobsters of Europe and North America.

Species *H. americanus*

This species is familiar to anyone who has eaten a lobster. Called the "Maine lobster," it is caught in traps from Canada to North Carolina.

FAMILY PAGURIDAE (puh-'gyu-ruh-dee)

Hermit crabs, without their borrowed snail shells, look a little like lobsters. They have long, twisted tails. Inside their foster homes, they look like crabs. They are neither, but more like something in between. Hermit crabs have soft, unprotected abdomens that can easily be pushed inside an empty snail shell. The problem occurs when these animals have to find new shells because they have grown too big for the old ones. Sometimes, when empty shells are scarce, they have been known to yank the snails out of their own shells so that they can have a place to live. Like the lobsters, they are carnivorous.

FAMILY   OCYPODIDAE (ō-'sipuh-di-dee) (swift-footed)

The ghost crab is a true crab because, unlike the lobster, shrimp, and hermit crab, this crustacean has a very small abdomen, or tail, which is tightly flexed under its body. Also, it doesn't have the flat, fanlike legs on the end of its tail like the lobster and hermit crab. Like other true crabs, the ghost crab runs sidewise, even though it can run rapidly in any direction.

In a related group, the fiddler crabs, only the males are equipped with large first claws (the claw on the other side is smaller), which they move back and forth or up and down to attract females to mate with them. Usually, the more vigorously they move their claws, and the larger the claws are, the more the opposite sex pays attention to their mating signals.

Class   CHILOPODA (ki-'lahpuh-duh)

Centipeds (100-legged worms) are swift-moving animals that are usually found hiding under logs or stones on land. Most have anywhere from 15 to 173 segments; each segment has one pair of legs, although the last two and the one behind the head (which bears a pair of poison claws for killing the food) do not. Even the long antennae have at least 12 segments.

Class   DIPLOPODA (deh-'plahp-uh-duh)

Millipeds, less active than the centipeds, move very slowly in dark, moist places, feeding on decaying organic matter on the ground. They have tubelike bodies. While they look like centipeds, most of their 25 to 100 or more segments have two pairs of legs, but no poison claws. They also have shorter antennae than centipeds. The legs on the males' seventh segment are used to insert sperm into the female.

Class INSECTA (ehn-'sektuh) (cut in)

Insects are, beyond any doubt, the most successful and most adaptable animals on earth. And the most influential, too. Some spread diseases, and many of them serve as food for other animals. A number of this group produces useful substances, like silk or honey. Without these insects, most of the flowering plants would never be able to grow their fruits and berries to make new plants.

It was during the Carboniferous period, about 345 million years ago, that insects became successful. Part of their success was due to their advanced body design; they could sense the environment and adapt to it better than the other creatures. Their success was also due to something no other animal had at the time: wings. Wings, which are really just outgrowths of skin strengthened by tubes of exoskeleton, provided not only a means of escape but also a way of spreading to other areas that couldn't be reached by crawling.

Insects have bodies that are divided into three separate parts that, in most animals, look like they were pulled slightly apart, then connected by thin segments.

An insect's head, which is made up of several small segments fused together, is filled with important sensing and feeding structures. There is one pair of antennae that may be used to touch, smell, or hear. Its two compound eyes, made up of dozens of tiny facets, are very good at detecting motion and, sometimes, color. And an insect has three pairs of mouthparts that were originally legs. In some species, the mouthparts are designed to do various things, such as biting or sucking. Other types of insects have crushing mouthparts or piercing ones.

The middle section, the thorax, contains the insect's legs

(three pairs) and the wings (one or two pairs). The legs are sometimes used for many functions, such as running, leaping, grasping, digging, or swimming. The abdomen has no legs on it. Usually, its only purpose is for mating and laying eggs.

There are at least 25 orders in this class.

Order   THYSANURA (thisuh-'nuruh)

Known as silverfish and bristletails, these are some of the most primitive animals in the insect class, mainly because they have no wings and because they go through no changes (except in size) as they grow. They have long, threadlike antennae, and long tails on the end of their abdomens. Both of these insects have chewing mouthparts, with jaws that are sunk into their heads.

Order   ORTHOPTERA (awr-'thahp-tuhruh) (straight wing)

Grasshoppers, crickets, "walking sticks," mantids, and cockroaches belong to this order. They are set apart from the other groups by their chewing mouthparts, their wings, and their legs. These creatures usually have two pairs of wings, if they have any at all. The front pair is thicker and narrower than the rear wings. They are not used to fly, but simply to cover the folded, fanlike rear wings when the animals are at rest. Their legs are designed for either jumping, crawling, running, or creeping.

FAMILY   PHASMIDAE ('faz-muh-dee) (apparitions)

Walking sticks—insects with long, narrow, sticklike bodies and legs—and leaf insects are slow-moving animals with colors and shapes that blend with the trees and bushes they feed on. Leaf insects have wings that exactly match the leaves surrounding them.

FAMILY   MANTIDAE ('man-tuh-dee)

Mantids are very helpful insects because they feed on

other insects that are harmful to crops. A mantid's tubelike thorax is very long. Attached to the front of it are two legs that are used as grasping arms and that can be bent to hold the mantid's prey. These insects blend very well with the grass due to their green-brown coloring. Because they lie in wait, with their grasping arms raised as if they were praying, they are usually called "praying mantids." After they have chewed their meal, they wash their faces the same way cats do.

FAMILY BLATTIDAE ('blad-uh-dee)

Cockroaches are a very ancient and highly successful group of insects. Most cockroach bodies are flat at the top and bottom and have long antennae. Their heads are bent down between their thoraxes. Most of them have wings, although they are rarely, if ever, used to fly. Cockroaches are fast runners and will eat nearly anything, especially garbage. Usually, they live under stones and sticks, but they also live in the crevices of people's homes.

Order ISOPTERA (ī-'sahp-tuhruh)

Wooden houses are one of the victims of the termites and white ants that bore through the wood with their chewing mouthparts. The wood is actually digested by protozoa swimming in the stomachs of these animals, leaving the nourishment for their hosts. Young termites, or nymphs, look almost like their parents, except that they lack the two pairs of long, narrow wings that lie flat on their backs when they are at rest. Isopterans live in large colonies under the ground or in huge mounds of dirt (especially in the tropics). Every member of the social colony has three purposes in life: to reproduce new termites, to get food, and to guard the colony against attack.

Order HEMIPTERA (he-'mip-tuhruh)

Bugs, such as the water boatmen, the back swimmers,

the giant water bugs, water striders, and leaf bugs, have mouthparts that pierce and suck and, usualiy, two pairs of wings. Their wings are different from the wings of the orthopterans because only the bottom half of the front wings are thick and leathery, but both the top parts of the front wings and the entire rear wings are light and thin. While many bugs are attackers of grain and vegetables, a few, like the bedbugs, can actually spread diseases.

FAMILY   GERRIDAE ('jer-rid-ee)

Gerridae, or water striders, do exactly what their name suggests; they rest their six slender legs on the surface of the water, using the water's surface tension to hold them up. They push their long bodies with their two middle legs. Most of them zip about on the surface of lakes and ponds at night, looking for dead insects to eat. Others stride for miles out in the ocean.

Order   ANOPLURA (anuh-'plurah)

Unlike fleas, which have long legs adapted for jumping, each of the anoplura, or sucking lice, has a single curved claw that helps it to cling onto the hair of its host. Sucking lice are wingless animals with very poor eyesight and even poorer roles in life. They are parasites of the skin of other animals, which they pierce and suck for nourishment. They also carry diseases, such as typhus. Lice glue their eggs, called nits, to the hairs of animals.

Order   COLEOPTERA (kolee-'ahp-tuh-ruh) (sheath-winged)

Beetles come in two varieties: some eat meat; others eat plants. But they both have mouthparts designed for chewing, and they both go through two stages—a larval and a pupa—before they become adults. Some are without wings, but the vast majority have two pairs of wings. The front wings, which are hard and thick, meet along the middle of their backs and cover the softer rear wings when the beetles are at rest.

FAMILY LAMPYRIDAE (lam-'piruh-dee)

Fireflies, or "lightning bugs," are active at night. They are soft-bodied creatures, about the size of a nickel, that have light-producing organs on the underside of their abdomens. Fireflies flash their lights as signals to bring both the males and the females together. Because the lights are so important for mating with their own species, each species has its own special signal. The larvae and the wingless females are called "glowworms."

Order LEPIDOPTERA (lepuh-'dahp-turuh) (scale wings)

Butterflies and moths are some of the most beautiful members of the insect group. For the most part, both moths and butterflies have two pairs of large, scale-covered wings, and they both go through two stages, larval and pupal, before becoming adults. The larvae, called caterpillars, have tiny antennae and chewing mouthparts because they feed on leaves and small insects. But the adults have sucking mouthparts that resemble long, thin tubes, which they curl up when at rest. The tubes are used to feed on the nectar of plants and juices of fruits.

Butterflies and moths differ in several ways. Moths, which are mostly active at night, have threadlike or featherlike antennae. Their colors are duller than butterflies, and their caterpillars usually spin silk cocoons around themselves. Butterflies, on the other hand, are mostly active during the day; their antennae have knobs on the ends. Their second stage, or pupae, hang from silken loops, and their wings are held vertically over their backs when they are at rest.

Order DIPTERA ('dipteruh)

Diptera are the true flies, which include such insects as mosquitoes, gnats, and houseflies. All have large antennae and big eyes. Most of them also have a pair of light wings for flying and a pair of tiny wings for balance. The mouthparts

Butterflies, like this Monarch, are active during the day. (U.S. DEPT. OF AGRICULTURE)

are either used for piercing and sucking or for licking. All of the flies go through a larval stage, where many of the larvae, called maggots, feed on a wide range of things, such as rotting wood, other insects, and animal excrement.

FAMILY CULICIDAE (kyu-'lisuh-dee)

Only the female mosquitoes suck blood. Mosquitoes breed in still water and lay their eggs there. For a time, the larvae live under water, sucking in the air on the water's surface with the siphons on the end of their abdomens. A few spread diseases—malaria, for instance.

FAMILY DROSOPHILIDAE (drō-'sahf-uh-luh-dee)

This group includes the tiny fruit flies.

Genus *Drosophila* (drō-'sahf-uh-luh)

Much of the information we have about heredity and genetics was gathered from experiments with these small fruit flies. *Drosophila* are usually found around rotting fruit in the summertime.

Order HYMENOPTERA (himuh-'nahp-tuhruh)

Taxonomists place the sawflies, ants, bees, and wasps in this order because they all have certain traits in common. Most hymenoptera have two pairs of delicate wings, which are held together on each side of their bodies by tiny hooks. The front pair of wings is slightly larger than the one behind it. Hymenoptera also have chewing or sucking mouthparts. If you examine a bee or wasp closely, you will see a very narrow waist that connects the thorax with the abdomen. Hymenoptera are unique in another way, too, because they have organs on the end of their abdomens that serve different functions for different families. This organ is called the oviposter, and it is used to bore holes in trees or in the bodies of other insects and to place eggs in these holes. It is also used as a stinger by the female bees and wasps.

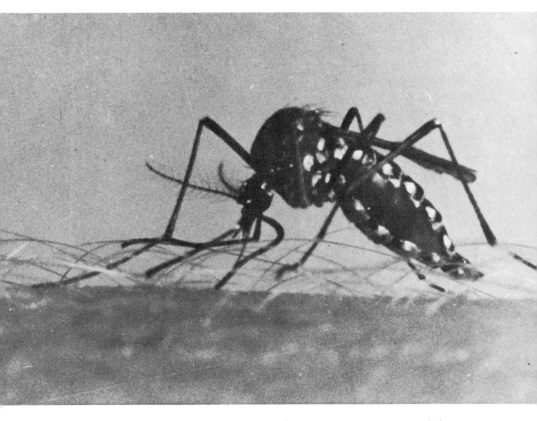

Mosquitoes, such as this yellow fever mosquito, can spread diseases.
(U.S. DEPARTMENT OF AGRICULTURE)

Most of these insects live solitary lives, but the rest, such as the termites, live in highly organized colonies.

FAMILY FORMICIDAE (fawr-'misuh-dee)

Most of the 3,500 species of ants are social insects and live in large colonies. They are thin-waisted, long-legged creatures, with good eyesight and two sets of jaws.

FAMILY APIDAE ('apuh-dee)

Honeybees pollinate flowers and have tongues that can lap up the flowers' nectar. The pollen they collect on their legs is later made into honey. Unlike wasps, these bees leave their stingers in their victims.

Class MEROSTOMATA (meruh-'stō-muhd-uh)

A number of the most ancient-looking arthropods belong to this class, some of which have been found in fossils at least 500 million years old.

The living species include all of the horseshoe crabs. They don't have antennae or jaws, but do have front pairs of small pincers. Their bodies are covered by two large plates of exoskeleton, which also end in long, pointed tails.

Order XIPHOSURA (zifuh-'suruh) (sword-tail)

Horseshoe crabs are marine animals found only on the east coast of Asia and North America. Although they are called crabs, they are really not crabs at all, but are more closely related to the scorpions and spiders. Horseshoe crabs usually burrow in the sand during the day, and their large, brown exoskeletons cover them like capes. They emerge from the sandy ocean bottom at night to feed on worms and mollusks.

Class ARACHNIDA (uh-'rak-nuh-duh)

The arachnida first arrived on this earth about 400 million years ago. Today, the group includes such varied crea-

Horseshoe crabs are not really crabs. They are related to the spiders.
(MARINE BIOLOGICAL LABORATORY)

tures as spiders, scorpions, harvestmen, mites, and ticks—to name a few. Arachnida have no jaws or antennae, but each has four pairs of walking legs, a pair of modified legs for sensing and handling food, and a pair of appendages around the mouth with which it handles prey. But in many spiders, these appendages are used as poison fangs. The head and the thorax of the arachnida are fused into one unit, but the abdomen is usually separated from the body by a narrow waist. However, this is not the case with mites and ticks. Their abdomens can't be separated from the rest of their bodies. Arachnida have simple eyes that are only sensitive to changes of light. They rely more on their sense of touch. Most of these animals drink liquid food that they squeeze and suck from their prey. They are also air-breathers; most cannot live under water.

Order SCORPIONIDA (skawr-pee-'ahn-uh-duh)

There are at least 700 species of scorpions living in the tropics and deserts of the world. They range anywhere from a ½ inch to 8 inches in length, and have eight eyes on their backs. What makes the scorpion stand out from the rest of the arachnids is the long slender tail that it holds up over its back when it walks. The tail ends with a stinger, but it is only used as a weapon of defense.

Scorpions hide in pits and cracks during the day, but are active at night, when they search for other insects and spiders. These they catch with their modified front legs, and they tear apart their prey with the appendages around their mouths. Most American species are harmless to people, although their sting can be painful.

Order PHALANGIDA (fuh-'lan-juh-duh)

Harvestmen, or "daddy longlegs," are not true spiders. They don't have silk glands, and, therefore, do not make webs or nests. Harvestmen have long, thin legs that are connected to bodies shaped like apple seeds. Much of the time,

Scorpions have no jaws, and their tails end with powerful stingers.
(U.S. DEPARTMENT OF AGRICULTURE)

these animals feed on small insects and the juices of fruits and vegetables. The adults mate in the fall and die soon afterward. Their eggs live through the winter and hatch in the spring.

Order ARANEIDA (or ARENEAE) (aruh-'nee-uh-duh)

There are seventy families of spiders, and their main claim to fame is a group of modified segments on the rear ends of their unsegmented abdomens. These segments, called spinnerets, are used for spinning silk. The silk is an amazing mass of fluid, which solidifies in air and is actually stronger and finer than anything man can produce. Spiders use their silk more for their egg cocoons and cables than for webs.

Spiders have well-developed nervous systems and even have memories. Their poison glands are open at the tips of the small appendages around their mouths, but spiders that net their prey do not use their poison. Only hunting spiders do this, although both species use poison for self-defense. But this weapon doesn't always help against their biggest enemy, the solitary wasp.

FAMILY THERIDIIDAE (theruh-'di-uh-dee)

These spiders are called the "comb-footed weavers" because each of their rear legs has a comb of curved, toothed bristles.

Genus *Latrodectus* (la-truh-'dek-tuhs)

Most of the spiders in this well-known genus are dangerous. Each is about the size of a dime, with a black body that is usually dotted with red. Its abdomen is round and glossy, and it has long, thin legs.

Species *L. mactans*

"Black-widows," are really not as bad as legend would have it. On one hand, they catch many harmful insects in

A "black widow" spider and its smaller male mate. (U.S. DEPARTMENT OF AGRICULTURE)

their thick webs; on the other, their bite is very painful. The female of the species is jet black, with a red hourglass design on the underside of her abdomen. The male—smaller and lighter in color—also has an hourglass figure on his abdomen. "Black-widows" are found in most of the United States, usually in trash, or in the cracks and crevices of buildings.

Class   PYCNOGONIDA (pik-nuh-'gahn-uh-duh)

Sea spiders, slow-moving predators of the ocean floor, feed on hydroids, sponges, anemones, and microscopic plants. From a slight distance, these tiny arthropods look like spiders. However, they are not, even though they have small bodies and long, thin legs. The sexes are separate, but the eggs are carried on the legs of the male.

Two
of a
Kind

7

PHYLUM

ECHINODERMATA (ekuh-nah-'der-muhd-uh)

(spiny-skinned)

Starfishes, sand dollars, sea cucumbers, sea urchins, and sea lilies are more closely related to the phylum to which people and other vertebrates belong: Chordata. The larvae of Echinodermata resemble the larvae of certain primitive members of the phylum Chordata.

Adult echinoderms are slow-moving creatures (if they move at all) that live mostly on the floor of the oceans and seas of the world. Scientists believe that at one time echinoderms or their ancestors were bilateral (having two sides that were mirror images of one another), but that their shapes changed when they became nonmoving individuals. Today they are radially symmetrical; that is, if you sliced them from their mouths down, each part would look identical. However, their larval forms still retain their original bilateral symmetry, which only changes when they are adults.

Most of these animals have internal skeletons that are made up of many lime plates embedded into their body walls. Within their skeletons they have well-developed body cavities somewhat like our own, that protect their internal organs from the movements of the body. They have a more modern digestive system than most other animals, but their blood system is poorly developed, and their nervous system is made up of only a net of nerves. They have no brains. But the characteristic that gives these animals their name is the many spines that usually project from their bodies.

Another unique trait these animals have is a water-vascular system—a complex of tubes and canals, filled with watery fluid. At first, water enters the body through a sievelike plate on the animal's surface. The water is channeled through a system of grooves and tubes into the echinoderm's feet. The feet are thin-walled hollow tubes that have suction cups on their ends. They are also one of the ways these animals get around. For animals like the starfish, these suction cups enable them to hold onto rocks or pull open bivalves, which they feed on.

The sexes of echinoderms are separate, and the eggs and sperm are released into the water.

Class ASTEROIDEA (astuh-'raw-deeuh)

Starfish have outer surfaces that are freckled with short spines. And they have numerous tiny jaws on their upper bodies. They also have arms that can grow back if they are cut off. A starfish's body is made up of a central disk, usually surrounded by five lobes (they are not really arms), each of which is covered with rows of tube feet along the middle of the lower surface. In the center of the lower surface is the mouth opening. The center of the upper surface has the anus and a short digestive tract runs between them. Starfish feed by actually pushing out the lower part of their stomachs through their mouths so that the animals are inside-out. When a starfish has successfully opened a bivalve with its tube feet and arms, it places its stomach over the soft parts of its prey. It then digests the bivalve, and sucks it up to its upper stomach. In order to breathe, the starfish has tiny gills that project outside its body wall. Also projecting outside its upper body are many jawlike structure that protect the gills and prevent any dirt from settling on the surface. These structures have been known to capture small prey.

Starfish feed on bivalves. They can grow new arms if they're cut off.
(NATIONAL OCEANIC AND ATMOSPHERIC ADMINISTRATION)

Order FORCIPULATA (fawr-sipyuh-'lahd-uh)

This group of starfish feed on bivalves, and have stalked, jawlike structures and big spines on their bodies.

FAMILY ASTERIIDAE (astuh-'rīuh-dee)

The five or more arms of these starfish—common to Europe and North America—taper to points. The animals have four rows of tube feet.

Genus *Asterias* (a-'stiree-uhs) (starred)

These common starfish of Europe and the eastern part of North America are usually found on rocks along the shore. They are most active at night.

Class OPHIUROIDEA (ahfee-yuh-'rawi-deeuh)

These animals, called brittle stars, serpent stars, and basket stars, look a bit like starfish, but they have major differences that set them apart from their relatives. Although they are equipped with five arms, the arms are longer, thinner, more flexible than the starfish, and many times branched into a number of smaller arms. Also, they do not use their tube feet for locomotion. Instead, they move by rapidly thrashing their arms. An ophiuroid also has a smaller disk than a starfish, and it breathes through pouches at the edge of it. This animal cannot push out its stomach, like starfish, and has no intestine or anus.

Brittle stars feed on minute organisms lying on the mud and scoop them into their mouths with their special tube feet. They are usually found under rocks in tidal pools. A few of this species live in deeper water, where they are luminous.

Class ECHINOIDEA (ekuh-'naw-deeuh)

Sea urchins and sand dollars are a bit like starfish. A sea urchin looks like a moving burr. Its skeleton is made up of

Sea urchins are related to the starfish. (NATIONAL OCEANIC AND ATMOSPHERIC ADMINISTRATION)

thousands of lime plates, packed together to form a near sphere. On the surface of the skeleton are usually long spines that wave and move the animals around. In some species, the spines are poisonous. Radiating up from the mouth, which is surrounded by teeth, are five rows of tube feet. They are longer and slenderer than those of starfish, and they must extend past the long spines to be effective for feeding on plants.

Sand dollars, on the other hand, are almost as flat as pancakes, and are covered with very short spines. They move about with their spines and tube feet, swallowing sand and digesting the organisms within it.

Class HOLOTHUROIDEA (halō-thuree-'awdeeuh)

A sea cucumber looks like the vegetable. It is a long, tubelike creature, with a fleshy body that is almost without the large skeletal plates of other echinoderms. It has no spines or jaws, but it does have ten branched tentacles around its mouth. Some even have tube feet.

Usually, a sea cucumber lies on one side of its body, with its anus on one end and its mouth (surrounded by tentacles) on the other. Most of these animals swallow mud and digest the organic material within it. Other species creep around, looking for better feeding grounds. Their average length is about eight inches.

Sea cucumbers may look pretty harmless lying in the mud, but to any crab or fish that may disturb them, they are not. They turn parts of their bodies inside out when they're touched. They spew out gobs of sticky thread from their glands and entangle and immobilize their predators. Then they lie in the mud and let their parts grow back.

PHYLUM

CHORDATA (kawr-'dahd-uh)

(having a cord)

To the scientists who study life's beginnings, what happened roughly 570 million years ago, in the waters of the Paleozoic era, is still a mystery. It was about that time that chordates arrived on this earth. How and why this happened is not altogether certain. But there are many theories. One particular theory seems to be accepted by many biologists. It was put forth by a famed Harvard University paleontologist, Alfred S. Romer.

Romer believed that the ancestors of both the echinoderms and the chordates had bodies like standing wineglasses. Long, feathery arms extended out from these stalked animals and swept the water, bringing down food to their gaping mouths. (This behavior and form can still be seen in the sea lilies of the echinoderms, the most primitive animals of that phylum.)

Although these creatures had an effective way of bringing their food down to their mouths, they were not very adept at getting the food from their mouths to their stomachs. Thus, gill slits evolved. This group of paired "slits," on either side of their throats, opened to the outside. They were surrounded by cilia, which drew water and food closer to the inside of the animals' bodies. Then, acting like strainers, they caught the food, passing the water back out through the slits. Thus they became filter-feeders. With the gill slits getting the food, there was no longer any need for the feathery arms or the stalks of their bodies, and these were gradually lost. (Many millions of years later, gill slits were used as breathing organs in primitive fish.)

That would have been the end of the evolutionary line; animals would have evolved into other sedentary filter-

Chordata Tree

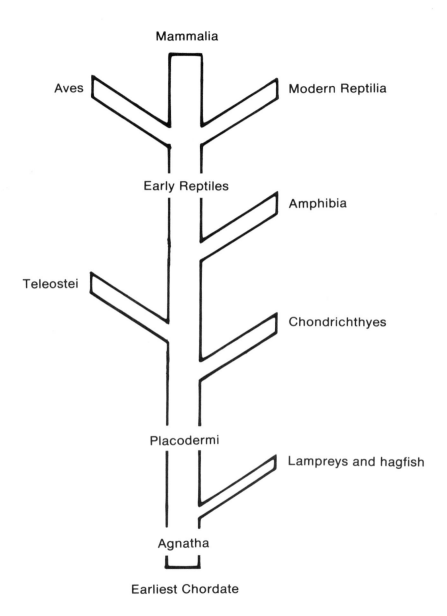

Mammalia

Aves

Modern Reptilia

Early Reptiles

Amphibia

Teleostei

Chondrichthyes

Placodermi

Lampreys and hagfish

Agnatha

Earliest Chordate

feeders, and fish, reptiles, and mammals would never have lived on this earth. But what saved the chordates from this fate was not another animal of the deep seas, but rather the larvae of these nonmobile, filter-feeding animals.

An animal that exists today, called the tunicate or sea squirt, is a chordate relative of that primitive filter-feeder of 570 million years ago. Sea squirts are not very inspiring to look at. They have tiny, shapeless bodies with two pipes, or siphons, sticking out of them. The pipes pull in the water and food to the gill slits and spew out the remaining water. Sea squirts remain attached to the rocks and pilings in shallow ocean water. Rarely, if ever, do they move from their positions. But they have a very mobile larvae. And it is the tiny ancestor of this larval stage that bore the first of the animals with backbones.

Actually, the larvae look like miniature adult sea squirts, except that the larvae have tails. But the tails are more complex than the flagella of simpler animals. Although the tails have muscles, the muscles by themselves are useless. They have to be attached to something hard and strong to pull against. Their tails are thus strengthened by long, flexible rods, called notochords. Still, this is not enough. Without any control over the muscles of the tail, the animal might travel in loops and circles, never getting anywhere. That is why the entire activity of the tail is controlled by a long, hollow nerve chord above the notochord.

The larval stage of the tunicates doesn't last very long. Once the adults spew out their larvae, they swim about for only a few hours, finally coming to rest on a rock or other solid place. Then they glue themselves to the spot, absorb their tails, and begin the life of a sedentary animal.

It was the same way with the ancestor of the chordates. It, too, had a larval stage when it looked something like a tadpole. But, somewhere along the line, while most of these larval forms attached themselves to rocks, a few rarely did. Through millions of years of changes, they no longer needed their adult forms to reproduce. They could do this in their mobile stages. Thus arose the beginnings of the first fish and the start of a new line of animals, the vertebrates.

Subphylum   VERTEBRATA (vuhr-duh-'brahd-uh)

Although animals like the tunicates are chordates, because they have notochords, gill slits, and hollow nerve cords, they are not vertebrates. Vertebrates, like ourselves, are only those animals that have backbones made up of a series of vertebra, or column of bones.

Animals with internal skeletons have an advantage over those that wear their skeletons around their bodies. For one thing, an internal skeleton can be very light and flexible, as well as strong. But an external skeleton must be thick if it is to have the same strength as an internal one. It can also be too bulky and stifle the mobility of an animal. This is one of the reasons why the vertebrates were so successful.

Class   AGNATHA ('ag-nuh-thuh) (jawless)

The first vertebrates that scientists have fossil records of were strange freshwater fish, called ostracoderms ('ahs-treh-kō-derms). They had large, thick plates of bone covering their heads and much of their bodies for protection against predators. They were jawless fishes, about a foot long (30 cm), and they spent most of their time scooping the bottom sediment through their permanently open mouths and filtering it through their gill slits. Ostracoderms didn't last long. From their beginnings about 450 million years ago, most finally died out some 350 million years ago. Lampreys and hagfish are the only living remnants of the ostracoderms.

Class   PLACODERMI (plakuh-'duhr-mī) (flat plate skin)

Placoderms began when the ostracoderms were starting to die out. Like the ostracoderms, they were heavily armored freshwater fish, but they had something the filter-feeders didn't have: jaws.

The bony gill bars, which protected the first gill slits on either side of the body, came together at their tips and became simple jaws. Eventually, these were the jaws that evolved in later animals. These fish died out after 50 million years.

Class CHONDRICHTHYES (kahn-'drik-thee-eez) (cartilage fish)

Before the placoderms died out, they had produced two new types of fish that were later to become very successful. They included the bony fishes and the cartilage fishes: sharks, skates, rays, and their relatives.

The skeleton of the chondrichthyes is—except for the notochord, teeth, and scales—totally made of cartilage, the same material that makes up the support of your ear. Apparently, like the lampreys and hagfish, sharks also lost the ability to make bone and had to fill in their skeleton with something that was almost as good: cartilage.

Beside having a skeleton made of cartilage, sharks, skates, rays, and their relatives have other traits that are not found in any other animals. For one thing, their teeth are really enlarged body scales that have migrated to the mouth. They are only set into the gums of the jaw, unlike our teeth, which are set into the jawbone.

A female chondrichthye fertilizes eggs within her body. The male has a device that is similar to the penis of mammals. It consists of a set of fins that have rolled themselves into a tube to transfer the sperm to the female.

Order SELACHII (seh-'lākeeī)

There are at least 250 species of sharks, but only a mere two dozen of them are dangerous to people. They are marine animals, having been that way ever since their ancestors left the lakes to swim into the oceans. At that time in history they were only about 3 feet long (1 m) and not yet the monsters of the sea. Today they are a very successful group of fish and are increasing in numbers.

The jaws of sharks seem to make everyone nervous when they enter the water, but the teeth of these animals usually interests the taxonomist. Each species has its own type of teeth. Some sharks that only eat crayfish off the bottom of the ocean have teeth that are no larger than grains of sand. Other sharks, which seize their prey with their jaws, have naillike teeth to hold onto their food. However, the teeth of all sharks are replaceable, and a single shark may go through a thousand teeth before it dies.

Sharks are not intelligent animals. A 10-foot shark may have a brain the size of a lemon. But it is very sensitive to its surroundings. Its two eyes can focus and see very clearly at night. And its ears can sense the slightest vibration. A shark's sense of smell can locate bleeding prey half a mile away, and the animal has an organ that can sense prey by the electrical signals the victim emits.

FAMILY   LAMNIDAE ('lamnuh-dee)

Mackerel sharks, porbeagles, and their relatives are large, fierce-looking creatures, with torpedolike bodies and large, triangular fins. They also have tail fins that are shaped like quarter moons. They are active hunters, and with their big mouths and large teeth, can swallow whole a good-sized fish.

Genus   *Carcharodon* (kahr-'karuh-dahn)

Perhaps the largest of the man-eating sharks are the white sharks. The descendants of sharks that were 30 feet long and had mouth openings larger than a standing basketball player, they may grow up to 20 feet or longer. White sharks have sharp, flat, triangular teeth, with serrated edges. The genus includes the Great White Shark.

Order   BATOIDEA (buh-'toideeuh) (flat fish)

The batoidea, or sawfish, skates, and rays, have broad, flat bodies and fins that are connected to them like capes.

Most of these fish feed off the bottom and have both their mouth and gill slits on the undersides of their bodies. When not buried in the sand, they swim, using the wavelike action of their wings (fins) to push them through the water.

Class OSTEICHTHYES (ahstee-'ikthee-eez) (bony fishes)

Most of the fish that you see in the ocean, lakes, and ponds are members of this class. Osteichthyes arose from the placoderms about the same time as the sharks. But, when the sharks were slowly losing their bone to cartilage, the osteichthyes were keeping and modifying the bones they had. One characteristic they developed was a thin, bony flap, called an operculum (ō-'puhr-kyuh-luhm, a lid). This covered the gill slits from the outside so that all of the water from the slits would be funneled out of one opening, and this made breathing easier. They also were covered with bony scales.

The other characteristic bony fishes developed was a pair of lungs. The earliest fishes already had gills, but the lakes and ponds they lived in sometimes ran out of oxygen. Gills didn't work very well when that happened. But with lungs (which were just pockets of the pharynx), fish could bob up to the water's surface and breathe air.

When the lungs evolved, the bony fishes split into two groups. One group, the lobe-finned fishes, who were the ancestors of the amphibians, used their lungs as much as their gills. The other group, the ray-finned fishes, modified their lungs into gas bladders, or air sacs which could be filled and deflated with air at will.

This led to a great number of different kinds of ray-finned fishes because they no longer had to keep swimming in order to stay at a particular level in the water. (All fish are denser than water and, therefore, tend to sink. For the sharks, it's literally sink or swim. With the gas bladders, ray-finned fishes were relieved of that problem.) They could now float without moving and didn't need to have bodies that were the least resistant to the flow of water (the least resistant shape is something like a torpedo—a shape that many sharks and fast-swimming fish have). It was because of this "invention" that the ray-finned fishes could develop into any shape imaginable.

Order   TELEOSTEI (telee-'ahstee-ī) (complete bone)

The teleosts were the result of that "invention." Today, there are well over 25,000 species of these animals, and they make up at least 95% of all the living species of fish. Nearly every fish you've ever seen or heard about is a member of this order. They come in all shapes, sizes, colors, and dispositions. They live in lakes, ponds, streams, and rivers; and some even take occasional strolls on land. They live at all levels—from the deepest parts of the ocean to just below the surface.

Probably because of their swim bladders, teleosts have smaller bones and less scales than other fishes (scales give less resistance to a swimming fish). For the most part, these animals have bones that extend to their fins (giving the fins support), which is why they can manipulate them so delicately.

FAMILY   CLUPEIDAE (klaw-'peeuh-dee)

This large family includes many of the fish that are served as hors d'oeuvres: herring, sardine, menhaden, and shad. They are soft-finned fish, with compressed bodies, forked tails, and very small teeth. They eat only the smallest life in the ocean—the plankton.

FAMILY   SALMONIDAE (sal-'mahn-uh-dee)

The Atlantic salmon and many freshwater trout belong to this family. They have large mouths and rounded, muscular bodies, which (except for the head) are covered with small, smooth-edged scales. Most of these animals live in the northern part of the northern hemisphere—usually in coastal waters. Almost all of them migrate from the ocean to spawn in the rivers where they were born. They are meat-eaters, and feed on insects, other fish, and crustaceans.

FAMILY   SYNGNATHIDAE (sin-'nathuh-dee)

This family's members are rather unusual looking. Their small bodies, protected by rings and ridges of bony plates, give them a stiff appearance. Their long, tubelike snouts have toothless mouths at the end. Most people know them as the pipefish and sea horse. Unlike most fish, the females of this family court the males. And the males incubate and protect the eggs in special pouches on their bodies. Sea horses are slow swimmers.

Genus   *Hippocampus* (kipuh-'kam-puhs)

These sea horses resemble the knights on a chessboard. They range from 2 inches to a foot in length. Most of them live in warm seas, in grasslike plants near the shore.

FAMILY   HETEROSOMATA (hed-uhrō-'sōmuhd-uh)

Flatfish, halibut, flounder, sole, and turbot spend most of their time lying on or buried in the sand. Their bodies are extremely flat and the upper sides are darker than the sides they lie on. Because of this, the fish have both of their eyes on one side of their heads, even though their larvae have them on both sides (the eyes move in development). They swim like a flat piece of paper with its edge against the wind, undulating their bodies slightly and settling back on the sand. They are also some of the most edible fishes in the sea.

Order   CROSSOPTERYGII (krah-sahp-tuh-'rijee-ī) (fringe fin)

Even though the ray-finned fish, like the teleosts, took over the oceans and lakes of the world with great success, it was the lobe-finned fishes, or crossopterygians, that scientists believe were the ancestors of the amphibians, reptiles, and mammals. The lobe-finned fishes lived roughly 350 million

The male sea horse carries the eggs. (AUSTRALIAN NEWS AND INFORMATION BUREAU: PHOTO BY J. KITZPATRICK)

years ago. They were freshwater fish with large, bony heads and bodies covered with scales. Instead of the thin fins of the teleosts, crossopterygians had thick, muscular stublike fins to move them about in the mud, when lakes and ponds dried up in the summer. Eventually, these fish died out (except for only one member, *Latimeria* that lives off the coast of Africa today), but one of their side branches lived on to become the first amphibian.

Class AMPHIBIA (am-'fib-eeuh) (leading a double life)

The first amphibians encountered many problems when they came on land. They were still very fishlike, spending most of their time in the water, where their heavy bodies were buoyant, and their lobed fins were able to move them around. But on land, where there was no buoyancy, their lobes were weak and their flexible notochord gave no support to their bodies. Gradually, bone replaced much of the notochord as hard vertebra, and the lobes became legs. But because they were placed too far up on the sides of their bodies, and their knees were pointed to the sides, the amphibians had to walk very slowly, while scraping their bellies on the ground. Salamanders still have this problem.

The other problem amphibians had to face was dryness. The animals have very tender skins and they fertilize their eggs outside their bodies. Therefore, if they're exposed to sun, their young dry up. That is why they placed their eggs in the water. Their larvae, the tadpoles, are aquatic.

An amphibian is cold-blooded; its body temperature changes with the temperature of the surrounding air. Moistness keeps its body cool. So the ancient amphibians, like the modern ones, were tied to the water. Because they never could leave the water completely to radiate to new land, most of them died out some 200 million years ago.

Order URODELA (yuruh-'deeluh) (visible tail)

Urodela, or salamanders, are four-legged amphibians

with tails, although some of these animals have no legs at all. They were one of the species that survived, and they look the closest to the ancient amphibians. Many of these animals can change their skin color to blend with the background. A few kinds of salamanders secrete a poisonous substance that leaves a bad taste in the mouths of their predators.

Most salamanders, if not in ponds or the edges of lakes, usually hide under logs and stones or in other moist places. There are no salamanders in the tropics, or in Australia, and very few in South America. Most of them live in North America. These amphibians eat insects as well as other small invertebrates.

Order   ANURA (uh-'nyu-ruh)

The earliest frogs had tails and spines with separate vertebrae. Somewhere along the line, jumping became part of their behavioral pattern, probably because it was the quickest way to escape from their enemies, and their bodies changed because of it.

Most frogs lay their eggs in fresh water. The larva, called tadpoles or polliwogs, have gills and long flat tails, and they spend much of their time feeding on plants in ponds. Most tadpoles only last a few weeks before they grow legs, lose their tails and gills, and walk on shore. But a few species, such as bullfrogs, spend several years in the tadpole stage.

Once the tadpoles become frogs, their food changes from plants to insects, earthworms, and spiders. They are able to catch these animals easily because they have tongues that they whip out of their mouths, and the sticky tips on their tongues can even adhere to flying bees.

Class   REPTILIA (rep-'til-eeuh) (the creepers)

The world of 250 million years ago was a harsh one for the amphibians. Many of them spent all or most of their lives in lakes and ponds that were filled with egg and larvae-eating predators, and that occasionally dried up during long, hot summers.

Originally, most amphibians laid their eggs in the water, where they were either eaten or killed when the water disappeared. But a few laid eggs that were not only individually surrounded by a shell, but also had food and a liquid environment in them. With this small, but very meaningful "invention," a few amphibians were able to escape their swimming predators and the droughts. They became the first reptiles.

Since that time, reptiles have adapted to life on land. Their skins became covered with bony scales; their legs grew stronger, and their knees moved so that they faced straight ahead. This gave them greater speed and lifted their bellies off the ground. Their vertebral columns became bonier and stronger, and their lungs and hearts became more suited to life on dry land. They fertilized their eggs within their bodies; their brains became bigger; their eyes grew eyelids for protection; and the bones of their necks gave their heads the ability to turn.

When the reptiles began to increase in numbers about 225 million years ago, they broke into several groups. There were the ichthyosaurs ('iktheeō-sors) and the plesiosaurs ('pleeuh-sors) that swam in the oceans; the therapsids (theh-'rapsehds) that eventually evolved the first mammals; the thecodonts ('theekuh-dahnts), which gave rise to the birds, and the dinosaurs. But about 65 million years ago, all of the dinosaurs and other primitive reptiles had vanished, leaving only the ancestors of the turtles, crocodiles, tuatara, lizards, and snakes. Like amphibians, reptiles are cold-blooded.

Order   CHELONIA (ke-'lōneeuh)

Turtles are easy to identify. All you have to do is look at their shells. But actually a "shell" is made up of two shells, an upper one and a lower one. They are both made up of dozens of bony plates covered with horny shields, and they are both connected to the turtle's skeleton.

Turtles live in fresh water, salt water, and on land. They

have toothless jaws, humanlike eyes, and necks that can retract into their shells.

Turtles are slow-moving animals, but they have life-
spans that are many times longer than other vertebrates. Because they are enclosed in an immovable shell, they can't
expand their lungs very easily, so they either have to move
their heads and thick limbs around to pull air in, or they
must gulp air.

Like most reptiles, turtles lay eggs, but they usually
make nests for them in soil or sand, even though they are not
cared for by the parents.

FAMILY   CHELONIIDAE (keluh-'nīuh-dee)

Cheloniidae, or large sea turtles have their legs modified
as flat paddles. They are abundant in the ocean. This group
includes the loggerhead, leatherback, and green turtles.

Genus   *Chelonia* (ke-'lōn-eeuh)

The green turtles swim in the warm waters of the Pacific
and Atlantic oceans, feeding on grasslike plants near the
shore. They are called green turtles because of the color of
their feet. Actually, they are brown.

During the spawning season, these animals come ashore
and lay their eggs in deep pits in the sand, above the high-
water mark. When the young hatch, they crawl out of the
sand in huge numbers and head for the sea. Those that are
not eaten by birds and crabs become adults.

Order   CROCODILIA (krahkuh-'dileeuh)

Crocodiles and alligators have changed very little since
they evolved some 200 million years ago. They have long
bodies and tails that are compressed from side to side. Their
legs are short and stumpy, and so are their necks. But they
can move around surprisingly well when they want to.

Crocodilians have several conelike teeth set into their
jaws. Female crocodilians lay their oval, hard-shelled eggs in

Sea turtles live most of their reptilian life under water. (STATE OF FLORIDA DEPARTMENT OF COMMERCE)

nests and guard them against predators. Both crocodiles and alligators are meat eaters and are usually found along tropical and subtropical lakes and marshes.

FAMILY CROCODYLIDAE (krah-kuh-'diluh-dee)

This group contains the true crocodiles.

Genus *Crocodylus*

Each crocodile has a pointed snout, and a tooth is exposed when the mouth is closed.

FAMILY ALLIGATORIDAE (aleh-guh-'toruh-dee)

This family contains the alligators.

Genus *Alligator*

Alligators have broad snouts, and no teeth are visible when their mouths are closed.

Order SQUAMATA (skwuh-'mahd-uh)

Lizards and snakes both belong to this order. They live in trees, on the ground, or in the water, and they both came from the same ancestor that lived 160 million years ago.

A lizard has a long body, with four legs and a tail (although some lizards don't have any legs at all). It also has good eyesight and sharp teeth. Usuallly, you can tell one lizard from another by looking at its digits, the shape of its limbs, the types and scales on its body, and the tongue. Every one of these characteristics is different for a particular species and is adapted to the environment in which the animal lives.

Male lizards are usually brightly colored and have broader heads than females. The females lay eggs and usually guard them. Most lizards eat plants. The rest are meat eaters.

Most snakes, on the other hand, eat meat only. They have long, tubelike bodies, without limbs, and they usually

Alligators feed along tropical and subtropical lakes and marshes.
(STATE OF FLORIDA DEPARTMENT OF COMMERCE)

shed their skins as they grow. Because snakes have no limbs, an adaptation that makes it easier to slide into the narrow holes of burrowing animals, they have to literally use their heads to catch their prey.

Snakes have keen senses. Because they are low on the ground, they are very sensitive to vibrations. They also have tongues that are sensitive to smells, and they can sense heat given off by another animal. Snakes can extend their jaws to swallow something twice or three times their own diameters. Most snakes are not poisonous. Those that are—usually the pit vipers—have sets of two hollow teeth that can inject poison into their prey. It is one of the most specialized and successful weapons that reptiles have. Most snakes lay eggs, but a few bear live young.

Class   AVES ('ā-veez)

Birds evolved from particular bird-reptiles, called *Archaeopteryx* (ahrkee-'ahptuh-riks), strange-looking animals with reptilian tails sparsely covered with feathers, and small, feathered wings. They probably glided more than they flew.

The modern birds that now span the globe are not very different from the early bird-reptiles. Their skulls, vertebrae, and feet are reptilian. So are their shelled eggs and the bony plates in their eyes, which protect their eyes from wind pressure. (In the primitive reptiles, the bony plates were a protection against water pressure.)

If there has been any change, it is in their use of wings. Birds have hollow bones and air sacs in their bodies to keep them light. And they have very large breastbones that are the main attachments for the muscles of their wings. The claw of a bird is unique, too. Most of the last half of the wing is actually supported by a tiny wrist and three fingers; the middle finger is fused together and grows thicker than the two fingers on the outer edges of the hand.

Birds are warm-blooded; that is, they have high and constant temperatures that are independent of their sur-

Birds evolved from reptiles. (STATE OF FLORIDA DEPARTMENT OF COMMERCE)

roundings. This requires a lot of energy to maintain. Not only do birds eat constantly, they also have excellent lungs, efficient circulatory systems, and four-chambered hearts like our own.

Most birds that fly, and many that don't, have excellent eyesight and larger brains than their reptile cousins. They can be taught to do tricks. But most species have set behaviors that are programmed in them before they are born. The majority of birds do not learn how to build nests or raise their young, because the parents are usually gone as soon as the young have learned to fly.

You can usually tell the occupation of each kind of bird by looking at its feet and beak, because they reflect what a bird eats and where it lives. Birds that paddle in the water have webbed feet; those that sit on the branches of trees and hunt for mice and snakes, have curled feet and sharp claws. Birds that eat hard-shelled nuts have short, powerful beaks, while birds that dine on worms usually have long, narrow beaks.

Many birds have voices. And many of the males have colorful plumage. These are usually used to attract mates of their own species, because each kind of bird has its own particular song or a particular plumage. No bird of one species will ever respond to the mating dance or song of another species.

Order   CHARADRIIFORMES (kuh-rad-reeuh-'formeez)

This group includes shore birds: gulls, auks, terns, and puffins. They are not colorful animals, usually having gray or brown feathers, but their bills and feet are bright orange. Most of these seabirds nest in colonies. Their eggs are laid on the ground, and the nestlings are already down-covered when they hatch.

FAMILY   LARIDAE ('la-ruh-dee)

The gulls and the terns.

Genus *Larus* ('la-ruhs)

Sea gulls are large, gray-feathered birds found around docks, piers, and fishing boats. Some of them are predators, but many of them are scavengers that eat the garbage people leave by the shore. Others often attack small birds and the eggs of other gulls. When they are excited or feeding, gulls utter harsh, screeching cries.

Order SPHENISCIFORMES (sfeh-nisuh-'for-meez)

Penguins, the most famous of the flightless birds, live in the southern hemisphere, usually in the colder sections of that part of the globe. But there is actually one species that lives on the Galapagos Islands, on the equator. These short-legged, stout-bodied birds range in length from the size of a duck to about 4 feet.

Penguins make their habitats with other penguins, building nests of stone and bits of vegetation. Most of them lay one to three eggs, and both parents help to incubate them.

They are excellent swimmers, using their wings like flippers, although they can only move them in circles. Their webbed feet are used for steering. Penguins feed on fish, krill, and squid.

Class MAMMALIA (muh-'māleeuh) (having breasts)

The first mammals, like the first birds, evolved from reptiles. They were small, ratlike creatures, with long snouts, and they probably fed on plants and insects.

Mammals were born in the age of the dinosaurs and, at first, were not very successful because they had to compete with the huge monsters. But when the dinosaurs died off some 70 million years ago, the mammals ruled the land and sea and evolved into the forms we see today. However, they could not have survived without having two things: their warm-bloodedness and improved methods of reproduction.

As we know, reptiles are cold-blooded animals that are inactive during the heat of the day and are active during the cool of the night. Because mammals had hair on their bodies to conserve their internal heat, they could remain active at all times of the day and year. They could also forage for food in regions that were too cold for reptiles. Gradually, because of their activity, mammals became more efficient, and their senses—especially hearing and smell—became highly developed. These improvements increased the size of their brains, and they became more intelligent.

Their teeth changed, too. Reptiles have teeth that are the same because they are usually only used for grabbing their food. But, because mammals were able to eat all kinds of food, their teeth modified to their diet. They had pointed teeth for grabbing, chisel-like teeth for slicing, and flat teeth for crushing.

The second reason for the mammals' success was their ability to reproduce. Because reptiles lay their eggs where they may be eaten by predators, many of the unprotected young that hatch do not survive. But most mammals keep their eggs inside their bodies until they emerge alive. Before that time, and in most mammals, the embryos (underdeveloped young) are nourished inside the mother by a special structure, the *placenta*. This connects the young to the mother's blood. The placenta not only protects the helpless young from predators, it also gives them a much longer time to grow. Once they are born, they are nourished and protected by the mother. The milk from her mammary glands is a ready source of food. Because the young are around their parents a lot, they can be taught what to eat and what to avoid.

Mammals are usually separated from one another by their eating habits, by the way they move around, or by the way they reproduce.

Order MARSUPIALIA (mahr-soopee-'āleeuh)

The marsupials are sometimes called "living fossils" because they are almost the same as they were 50 million years ago. Marsupials—including the pouched kangaroos, wombats, koala bears, and opossums—are different from other mammals because their young, although born alive, are still underdeveloped.

When these tiny young emerge from their mothers, they crawl up to their mother's stomach and into a pouch attached to it. Then they place their mouths over their mother's mammary nipples, and stay in that position until their development is complete. This is not a very successful way of rearing young, and there are not very many of these strange animals because of it.

Marsupials live in trees, close to the water, or on the ground. Most of them are found in Australia, South America, and New Zealand, but a few are natural inhabitants of the United States.

FAMILY DIDELPHIDAE (dī-'delfuh-dee)

When the young of opossums emerge from their mothers, they are so small that their bodies can easily be placed into the body of a bumblebee. The only part of an opossum's body that is not underdeveloped is its forelimbs, because it has to use them to pull its tiny bulk to its mother's pouch. An adult opossum has short limbs—four feet with five distinct fingers on each one. It also has a long, naked tail that it uses to grasp, wrap around, or seize objects. Its head is cone-shaped, and it has a pointed snout and beady eyes. The fur is coarse and long.

Opossums are unsociable creatures, staying out of the way of most people. But when they are cornered, they play dead ("play possum"), and usually remain this way for several hours.

Order INSECTIVORA (in-sek-'tiv-uhruh) (insect eaters)

The insectivors—the moles and shrews—are the most primitive of the mammals with placentas. They show traits that were part of the earliest mammals many millions of years ago. Moles and shrews have stumpy little bodies, long snouts that reach beyond their mouths, beady eyes, and slender heads. They usually feed on insects, but some eat vertebrates. Most insectivors are found throughout the world, with the exception of Australia, Greenland, and southern South America.

Order CHIROPTERA (kī-'rahp-tuhruh) (finger wings)

Bats are the only mammals that can fly. They have long, slender fingers, covered by sheets of leathery skin. The skin connects to their sides, legs, and tails to make a wing.

These furry animals have unusual ways of flying in their surroundings and in finding food. They produce short, high-pitched sounds out of their mouths or noses, which bounce off objects and come back to their very large ears. The method is called *echolocation*.

Bats are not blind, but they usually rely more on sound than sight because their echolocation is very accurate at night, when they hunt for food. Most people think that bats eat insects only. But there are bats that eat meat, and some (vampire bats) that suck blood. Other species eat only fruit.

Order LAGOMORPHA (laguh-'morfuh)

Rabbits, pikas, and hares, are land animals noted for their two pairs of large front teeth and their way of getting around. They are plant eaters, and their teeth are designed to cut and scrape their food. Lagomorphans use their feet for hopping, but when they are running, they use their toes.

FAMILY LEPORIDAE (luh-'poruh-dee)

This group is made up of rabbits and hares. Hares are born with fur on their bodies and with their eyes wide open. They prefer rock crevices for cover. Hares are larger, with longer ears and limbs than rabbits. They are also excellent runners.

Rabbits, on the other hand, are born hairless, with their eyes closed. They prefer burrows and the undersides of logs and tree roots for homes. They have short legs, and are not very strong runners.

Order ROTENTIA (ro-'denche-uh) (the gnawers)

Rats, mice, squirrels, gophers, beavers, and porcupines belong to this order. They all have large, chisel-like teeth in the front of their mouths that grow constantly. One of the reasons why they gnaw is to keep their teeth sharp and to prevent them from growing too big.

Rodents have invaded almost every environment. Some live in trees, and some in burrows; others live most of their lives by the water or in it. Some rodents are meat eaters, and some are plant eaters. They are most active at night, and they tend to reproduce in large numbers.

FAMILY CASTORIDAE (ka-'storuh-dee)

Beavers are the largest rodents in North America. They have heads that are broad and round, bodies equipped with powerful muscles, and short legs with webbed feet. Their large, flat tails help them to regulate their body temperatures and to store fat. Their tails also serve as rudders when they swim in the water. Beavers build dams and burrows, which they use as homes. Large dams are usually the work of many generations of beavers.

FAMILY MURIDAE ('myuruh-dee)

This group includes the Old World (found on the continent of Europe) rats and mice. The most successful of the rodents, they have three cheek teeth, above, below, and on each side of their jaws. They do not have any cheek pouches (that normally store food in other rodents).

Genus *Rattus* ('rad-uhs)

The most numerous and variable of the mammals, these Old World rats have coarse fur, and long thin tails. The average rat often grows as large as a domestic cat.

Species *R. norvegicus*

The Norway rat arrived in North America by way of the first ships to land on the continent. In the late 1700s, they began to spread throughout the country. Today, most live wherever there is a lot of food—in dumps, in restaurants, and in sewers.

Norway rats are excellent swimmers, divers, climbers, and burrowers, and they are very active at night. They have poor eyesight, but excellent smell and hearing. Like the bats, they can even use echolocation. During the fourteenth century, these rats were partly responsible for spreading the disease known as the "black death" (bubonic plague), because they carried fleas containing harmful parasites. Twenty-five million Europeans died of the plague.

Order CETACEA (see-'tasheeuh)

Millions of years ago, mammals with four legs left the land to become creatures of the water. Today, they are the whales, dolphins, porpoises, and other aquatic mammals that live in the rivers, lakes, and oceans of the world.

Cetaceans have bodies that are adapted to the water, but they are still air-breathing mammals that must stick their nostrils out of the water every once in a while or they would drown. All of this group have torpedo-shaped bodies, forelimbs that have been modified into flippers (without claws), and tails that have been flattened side-to-side to become flukes (which are directed horizontally, unlike the shark's tail, which operates in a vertical direction). Most cetaceans have no sweat glands, and their skins are smooth and virtually hairless. Unlike humans, cetaceans' windpipes are connected from their lungs to their nostrils, or blowholes.

Cetaceans have fatty deposits on top of their heads called melons. In many of the mammals, these melons are used as aids in echolocation.

Order CARNIVORA (kahr-'niv-ehruh)

Carnivors include cats, dogs, weasels, bears, seals, and

Carnivores, like this cat, have large canine teeth for stabbing their prey. (STATE OF FLORIDA DEPARTMENT OF COMMERCE)

The wolf, Canis lupus, is related to the domestic dog. (TONY MICHAELS, WILD CANID SURVIVAL AND RESEARCH CENTER—WOLF SANCTUARY, ST. LOUIS, MO)

walruses. They are designed to hunt meat, and usually have sharp claws and long, conelike, pointed canine teeth which are used for seizing and stabbing their prey. All of their other teeth are sharp, too, and some of them act like scissor blades.

Most carnivors bear one or two litters every year. The young, usually born helpless, are cared for by their mother or by both parents.

FAMILY CANIDAE ('kanuh-dee)

Coyotes, wolves, foxes, and some dogs are lithe, muscular animals, with long muzzles, large, pointed ears, and long, bushy tails. Besides being highly intelligent, alert, and cunning, they are armed with long, slightly curved canines. Most of these long-limbed animals are fast runners.

Genus *Canis* ('kā-nehs)

Some dogs and wolves have large, erect ears and long bushy tails. Such species also have a line of long hairs—extending from the middle of the neck to the shoulders—which forms a mane and stands erect when the animal is ready to fight.

Species *C. lupus*

The gray wolf is a relatively large animal, with a long, bushy tail. It usually has a gray, or brown-and-black coat and white underside. With its long, pointed muzzle and long legs, it almost looks like a large German Shepherd dog. But dogs and wolves are different in several ways. Dogs carry their tails high; wolves carry their tails low. Their tracks are also different.

Order ARTIODACTYLA (ahrd-eeuh-'dak-tuh-luh)

This order of ungulates, or hoofed mammals, has only two toes on which it stands. The reason these animals stand on their toes is because there is much better leverage and bounce on the toes than on the flat foot. The fastest animals

Cattle belong to the order Artiodactyla and stand on only two toes.
(BILL BROWNING, MONTANA CHAMBER OF COMMERCE)

Horses stand on only one toe. (STATE OF FLORIDA DEPARTMENT OF COMMERCE)

are usually those that run either on all their toes or on one toe.

The hoofed animals include the hippopotamuses, camels, giraffes, deer, sheep, cattle, bison, and pronghorn antelopes. They are usually plant eaters that browse or graze in fields. Most chew their cuds—actually a process of eating, swallowing, regurgitating, then re-eating the same food again and again so that it can be broken down enough to be digested in the stomach.

Order   PERISSODACTYLA (puh-'risuh-'daktiluh)

These animals usually stand on just one large toe. They include horses, zebras, tapirs, and rhinoceroses.

Why We're Here

8

Order PRIMATES (prī-'māt-eez) (one of the first)

Monkeys and apes are mammals that belong to the class that includes deer, dogs, whales, and moles. But somehow, by looking at their faces and expressions and watching their behavior in zoos and in nature, we get the feeling they really are special and separate from the other mammals. After all, they look and act a little like us, don't they? Well, they should. We *are* their closest relatives. This is why an entire chapter has been devoted to them and to us.

The greatest influence in the development of the earliest primates was not another animal, but the tree. The first primates lived in trees because they were safe from their largest predators, the carnivores. But the primates weren't very well suited to live in trees. Even though they had tails (called prehensile tails) they could wrap around branches, their arms and legs were not really made to swing to other limbs, and the digits on their paws were stiff and awkward. But these things changed in their descendants.

The first change was in their body structure. The earliest primates had limbs like a dog; they could easily move backward and forward, but not from side to side. But the later primates developed shoulder joints that gave their arms freedom to move in any direction, and elbow joints that gave them even more rotation. While most other mammals were losing their collarbones (the bones just under the neck and across the shoulders), the primates kept theirs. Because the collarbone is an attachment place for the muscles of the upper arms, this was a very important modification for the primates' tree life. They now had arms that enabled them to swing from branch to branch and they also had strong muscles that gave them more power.

The other change in their structure was in their digits. Having the freedom of their arms was no good unless they could grab onto branches. Therefore, they kept all of their digits (unlike the horses and pigs), and this gave them more mobility. Evolution also reduced their claws to mere nails and gave them touch pads on their fingertips for greater sensitivity. But the biggest improvement in their paws came when they developed thumbs and big toes that moved opposite to the other four digits. This gave them much more grasping power.

The original primates had eyes, like the eyes of other mammals, on the two sides of their heads. But when the eyes migrated to the front of their faces, it gave them perception of depth and distance—a very important asset when they were swinging for branches yards away. And with their eyes and the movements of their arms and legs now developed, their brains enlarged.

All of these developments, plus the reduction of their snouts, their two mammary glands, and the birth of only one young per pregnancy, were caused almost entirely by their tree-dwelling environments.

FAMILY   LEMURIFORMES (luh-myuruh-'for-meez)

The lemurs—found only on the island of Madagascar, off the east coast of Africa—are one of the more primitive primates. They are rather small tree dwellers, with long, wolflike snouts and bushy tails. But they are primates because they have thumbs and big toes that oppose the other digits and are equipped with fingernails.

FAMILY CEBIDAE ('sebuh-dee)

This group of New World monkeys includes the "organ-grinder" monkeys, spider monkeys, and squirrel monkeys. All have nostrils that are pointed to the sides of their faces. Most of them have prehensile tails that grasp or wrap around an object like an arm.

FAMILY CERCOPITHECIDAE (suhr-kō-peh-'theesuh-dee)

The baboons, mandrills, and macaques (rhesus monkeys) are called the "Old World" monkeys. Their tails are not prehensile and their nostrils are not separated like those of the New World monkeys. Instead, their snouts are pointed forward and down. Usually, these animals have brightly colored areas on their buttocks, which function like seat cushions and as sex attractants for the females.

FAMILY PONGIDAE ('pahn-juh-dee)

These tailless large primates are called the "great apes." They include the gibbons, orangutans, gorillas, and chimpanzees. Most of them have very long arms and large skulls and brains. They walk on all fours, and use the knuckles of their hands as supports.

FAMILY HOMINIDAE (hō-'minuh-dee)

The ancestors of the hominids probably left the trees when the forests they lived in slowly opened up into fields of tall grass. The animals were still adapted to the trees at the time, and probably found it difficult to survive. Their greatest enemies, the carnivores, were already well adapted to hunting on land. But the hominids survived because of their intelligence and their thumbs, which made it easier to construct crude weapons and grab for food. Gradually, though, they began to look less apelike, and lost their crouched stances. They started walking on two legs. Their arms, teeth, and jaws grew shorter. And their brains grew larger until they were no longer monkeys but intelligent, toolmaking human beings.

Genus *Homo*

Called "modern man," this being has a large braincase and a very high intelligence. Unlike the animals of the earth, man can modify and, in some cases, control the environment in which he lives, and alter the future.

Species *H. sapiens*

The only living species of the genus *Homo*, modern man lives all over the world and embodies many different races, which can all interbreed. *H. sapiens* is the only species that has the capability of destroying itself, or changing its form through the genetic engineering of its cells.

In one or two million years from now, species *Homo sapiens* may not be around. Neither may any of the other species. We have seen what a few million years of evolution has done to a group of animals. They have been gradually replaced by species better able to adapt to the environment. This may happen to our own species. But it is impossible to foresee what that new species will look like. We can only hope that we will not destroy ourselves and the life around us before that time arrives. Otherwise, the taxonomy book of one or two million years or so from now may place our group in an entirely different phylum.

Index